The Theology of Canon Law

The Theology of Canon Law

A Methodological Question

by Eugenio Corecco
translated by Francesco Turvasi

Duquesne University Press
Pittsburgh, Pennsylvania

Published in French under the title
Théologie du Droit Canon

English Translation
Copyright © 1992 by Duquesne University Press
All Rights Reserved.

Published in the United States of America

by Duquesne University Press
600 Forbes Avenue
Pittsburgh, PA 15282–0101

Library of Congress Cataloging-in-Publication Data
Corecco, Eugenio.
    [Théologie du droit canon. French]
    The theology of Canon law: a methodological
    question / Eugenio Corecco;
translated by Francesco Turvasi.
        p.   cm
    Translation of: Théologie du droit canon.
    Includes bibliographical references (p.   ) and index.
    ISBN 0-8207-0238-2
    1. Law (Theology)—History of doctrines.   2. Law—
    Philosophy—History.   3. Christianity and law—
    History.   4. Canon law—History.
    I. Title.
    BT96.2.C67   1992
    262.9—dc20   91–38559
                                                       CIP

Contents

Contents

Contents

Acknowledgments

I wish to express my deep gratitude to the Pontifical College Josephinum, whose faculty has given great support to the publication of this volume. In particular, I am grateful to Fr. Donald Nesti, C.S.Sp., Professor of Systematic Theology, for introducing my text to the publisher; to Fr. Arthur Espelage, O.F.M., Professor of Canon Law, for his expertise in reviewing the text; and to Fr. Francesco Turvasi, M.S.C., Professor of Dogmatic Theology, for preparing the English edition.

— December 1991
Eugenio Corecco

1

The Phenomenological Experience

In our human experience, law is perceived as an external reality that limits our personal freedom and autonomy. In our daily lives, we feel law to be the coercive force of the organized system of power. Thus, law seems to be a manipulable reality, a reality that is determined by the will of powerful and diverse ideological groups, a reality that is frequently the expression of the will of intolerant special interest groups. From the phenomenological perspective, moreover, law manifests itself as a nonunitary reality. Its norms — whether their source is the state or an association, religious or worldly, national or international; and whether dictated by positive law or by custom — are frequently heterogeneous, and these norms may also reveal themselves to be unjust.

Our human experience of the law includes both

1

this negative aspect and a positive one. In addition to limiting our own freedom, law is also the indispensable instrument for maintaining social living and for guaranteeing order and peace, because it imposes limits on others. Therefore, law shows itself to be a crucially important social factor, as it allows both individuals and the community to confidently plan for the future, knowing we are protected by juridical continuity and certainty. Not only is law perceived as the expression of a heteronomous will, then, but also as an element of equilibrium; we experience the juridicial phenomenon as representing the will of the strongest, but also as something that transcends individual interests — as justice.

These negative and positive elements of law are superimposed upon one another. This explains the perception that law is a paradoxical experience (WOLF), embodying apparently contradictory values that cannot be severed from one another. The negative aspects of this primordial experience of law have repeatedly given rise to the sociopolitical phenomenon of anarchy, while the experience of law's positive aspects has constantly been contained by the limits of law's utopian and *ad absurdum* dynamic.

The experience of canon law often places the Christian in a paradoxical situation (ROUCO VARELA). The confession of faith — which involves all of a person's life, to the very root of personal freedom — is bound by canonical norms. Divine law, although also manifested in prophecy and charisms, must be subjected to the interpretation of human law if it is to assume any *concrete* historical position. Though it still remains the law of the mystical Body, this law takes on associational or state forms that often cannot express the profound theological truth and nature of ecclesial communion. The law becomes one both of love and of institution, of freedom and of limitation, of divine and of human justice — both of Gospel and of Law. Thus, the term *canonical* frequently evokes the idea of conformism, while *continuity* or *judicial certainty* calls to mind the idea of preserving the status quo. Law seems to be, then, the greatest obstacle to dynamic manifestations of the Spirit. Consequently, law becomes an impediment to the missionary nature of the Church, which otherwise stands ready to respond to the changes and claims of our present sociocultural reality.

The positive elements of the "canonical" experience, however, are fundamental to the Christian experience, both on an individual and a community level. Canonical discipline guarantees the unity of the symbols of faith, of the Sacraments, of the preaching of the Word, of the ecclesial constitution. Canonical discipline also guarantees the objectivity of the ecclesial experience, as it teaches individual Christians and churches that they must overcome the temptation of individualism and that fidelity to communion is essential for the self-realization of the Church. According to canon law, then, the possibility that the Spirit of the Lord will show itself through charism, divorced from all objective bonds, is a utopian view.

During the course of history, the paradoxical nature of the canonical experience has provided fuel for all the spiritualistic movements — Montanist, Cathar, Franciscan, Hussite — that anticipated the tensions that exploded in the Protestant Reformation. Allowing itself to be overcome by the same spiritualistic temptation, Protestantism soon subdivided into a multitude of sects; its spiritualism often prevented the Protestant movement from guaranteeing the degree of objectivity necessary for a fully ecclesial reality.

The experience of law — whether secular or canonical — has been characterized by conflicts between the relative and the absolute, the contingent and the transcendent, the particular and the universal, history and eschatology. It was inevitable that this paradoxical human experience, through its heterogeneity, should stimulate philosophical and theological reflection on the nature, origin, and intrinsic unity of the juridical phenomenon. The problem of the unity of law has become central to the Christian philosophy of law and to the theology of canon law. Is there indeed a connection between the often precarious law that governs the social cohabitation of human beings and some set of divine norms? And can we rely upon such divine law to be confident that human systems are just and based on solid foundations?

2

The Unity of Law in Christian Philosophical Thought

PREMISES IN GRECO-ROMAN PHILOSOPHICAL THOUGHT

The need to find a unitary explanation for the juridical phenomenon emerged early in the Greek conscience. Greek culture was deeply rooted in the mythical, the sacred, and in aristocracy; within this cultural milieu, the Greeks accepted the idea of the unicity of law. Law *(themis)* is understood by Homer as the sacred decree of the gods, revealed to the kings and the upper class. The aristocracy is then also given the task of preserving the law. Even as a proper system of human legislation is progressively

5

added, justice (*diké*) continues to be seen primarily
as a divine instrument rather than a human reality.
In the poetical version of Hesiod, when the human
judges pronounce unjust sentences, Dike sits next
to her father, Zeus, and tearfully recounts to him
the wicked thoughts of human beings.

The idea that an absolute foundation for positive laws existed — as a way of relating the
state's positive laws to a dependence on superior
norms — was first defined in Greek tragedy in the
fifth century B.C. In Sophocles' *Antigone* (ca. 405
B.C.), the heroine accepts death rather than dis-
obey those "unwritten laws" that are superior and
divine, eternal and immutable. Those who argue
for the existence of an absolute and supreme foundation for human laws have traditionally seen this
as the earliest example of the concept of *natural
law* in the Greek conscience (FASSÒ).

We need not ask whether pre-Socratic philosophy
offered a transposition from the cosmic order to a
social and juridical one (VERDROSS) or, on the contrary, from the proper human ethical-political experience to the order of the physical universe. This
physical order was sometimes even conceived as a
"democratic" order (*isonomia*). We must note, however, that the fundamental preoccupation of the
pre-Socratic philosophy was that a connection
should at least be established between the cosmic
and the social orders, even when the specific issue
of their intrinsic interdependence — that is, of the
unity of law — was not yet an explicit concern. This
preoccupation is already present in Parmenides
(early fifth century B.C.) when he affirms that not
only is it absolutely necessary for cosmic reality to

be always equal to itself, but also an ethical-juridical reality "must be" present on the level of social relations. The same preoccupation with discovering a principle to unify all orders of reality dominates the thought of Pythagoras (b. ca. 582 B.C.) for whom both the harmonic order of the physical world and the virtue of justice are ruled by a mathematical relation and, therefore, by a single rational principle (STEFFES).

Heraclitus (b. ca. 500 B.C.) accuses Homer and Hesiod of having anthropomorphized divinity and argues against Pythagoras by pointing to the experience of a visible world dominated by an unrelenting and merciless struggle of all beings (*polemos*). Unlike Democritus and Epicurus, however, he does not reduce visible reality to a phenomenon of accidental aggregation deprived of providential or rational order; he still holds that, behind the reality of beings — which is continuously fluid in its becoming — there is a hidden harmony. This harmony is guaranteed by the eternal *logos* which, for Heraclitus, is to be pantheistically identified with God or, at least, with a divine emanation (VERDROSS). Since this universal reason is the ordering principle of all cosmic reality, it is also the foundation of human social life. There is no sphere of justice because all human laws (*nomoi*) are contained within a harmony that places them within a superior unity: "All human laws feed on a single divine law" (*Fr.* 114). Nevertheless, Heraclitus does not define the intrinsic nature of the connection that unifies the hidden and the visible realities. He limits himself to the affirmation that humans can discover the divine *logos*, substance and principle of all reality, in the depth of the psyche by means of philosophy, through which we go "from sleep into wakefulness."

The Unity of Law and the Stoic Concept of Nature

The first great shift from an objective to a subjective reality came after the time of Alexander the Great (d. 323 B.C.), with the Greek civilization founded on the *polis* evolving toward Hellenistic cosmopolitanism. The individual, having been divested of the total ethical-political commitment of the city-state, could now profess a more tranquil and serene ideal of life (*ataraxia*) (FASSÒ). In accordance with this new cultural situation, Epicurus (d. 270 B.C.) posits the "true nature of man" as the foundation of all philosophical thought; this nature is described as being constituted by the instinct for pleasure, power and individualism. The "naturally just" is no longer sought in a reality that is autonomous and external to human reality but in that which humans contractually decide in light of their own interests. This subjectivist tendency, which might have resulted in a destructive positivism, does not go so far as to break the unity of law. Human laws, by intrinsic necessity, still need to be elaborated by reference to that objective reality that is the "true nature" of human beings (FLÜCKIGER).

With Stoicism's introduction of a new psychological element, Greek philosophy moves further away from the traditional objectivist view. The sense of the just and the unjust is no longer considered an instinctive predisposition, as in Epicurus, but as a rational and innate human characteristic. The maxim of Zeno (d. 430 B.C.), "to live in conformity with one's own self," or "with nature" (CLEANS, d. 223 B.C.), provided the basis for this new philosophical current (WENZEL). The rational predisposition of human beings coincides with nature, or with the universal and necessary law ruling the cosmos; this law is in turn identified with the divine, which pervades the world by forces corresponding to the several orders: the organic order by *physis*, the animal by *psyche* and the human by *logos* (STIEGLER). In our own rational nature, we humans find already preordained moral and the juridical norms. The unity of law is formally preserved by the affirmation that human law must be a positive translation of universal reason. This unity ultimately remains abstract and extrinsic, however, because universal reason neither imposes nor requires the abolition of social and juridical differences existing among people. Our awareness of membership in a spiritual kingdom that cannot be taken away from us does not depend on our concrete political situations (VERDROSS).

With Chrysippus (d. 207), a concept of law (*nomos*) appears that seems to be superior to the Heraclitean *logos*. This refers to the universal reason which guides the course of all things, human and divine, with the same logic of strict necessity proper to destiny; indeed this universal reason is to be identified with destiny. *Nomos* becomes a third form of law attached to the traditional distinction of Greek philosophy between natural (or divine) and positive law; Chrysippus calls the latter no longer *nomos* but *thesis*.

The yet unclear trilogy, which had perhaps already

surfaced in Aristotle, is articulated more clearly in the teaching of Cicero (d. 43 A.D.) concerning the *lex aeterna*. Both the law of nature, which rules nonrational beings, and the ethical-juridical or natural law, which defines good and evil, depend upon right reason. Ethical-juridical law does not exist exclusively in the divine spirit; it also manifests itself in our human reason. In other words, we do not come to know law empirically or on the basis of its positive expressions, but we discover law in our own human nature. Despite its pantheistic elements, the doctrine of *lex aeterna*, because of its intrinsic unity, was filtered through Lactanicus and Augustine and carried into the Christian theological system as it moved to establish a connection among *ius divinum, ius naturale,* and *ius humanum* (FASSÒ).

Fascination with the concept of *lex aeterna* led Seneca (d. 65 A.D.) to affirm that even the Creator and Ruler of the universe is subject to the higher law of rational necessity. This view gives rise to the dilemma of the relationship between the reality of things and God's freedom; this dilemma, more than a millennium later, forms the basis for the dispute between voluntarism and intellectualism (STIEGLER).

In Greece, the problem of law, generally faced in the context of the study of ethics, had remained in the domain of the philosophers. In Rome, where jurisprudence and the doctrinal elaboration of law reached the highest peaks of perfection, law became the perogative of jurists who were predominantly under the influence of Stoicism. In place of the traditional distinction *physis/nomos*, already undermined by the Ciceronian *lex aeterna*, late Roman jurists formulated the trilogy *ius naturale, ius gentium,* and *ius civile.* The *ius naturale* was at times defined according to rationalistic criteria, as by Julius Paulus (early third century A.D.), and at other times according to naturalistic criteria, as by Ulpian (d. 228). This law was no longer considered to be an absolute and abstract law placed outside history, in the way Greek natural law philosophy had defined it, but was an actually existing law, practiced by nations and not bound to absolute metaphysical presuppositions (FASSÒ). Gaius (second century A.D.) defined the *ius gentium,* insofar as it is applied among all nations, as the law that "natural reason establishes for all [people]." By this definition, he established a parallel with natural law, which, for Stoicism, was defined as a norm dictated by reason. Therefore, it became inevitable that *ius naturale* and *ius gentium* should be ever more frequently confused with each other until Justinian (565 A.D.), in the *Institutiones,* established the relationship between the two.

The problem of the unity of law was not posed in philosophical terms by the Romans, but in concrete and pragmatic ones. They never held natural law to be superior to or more valid than the *ius gentium* or to the *ius civile* (prerogative of each state) because all three coincide in being a form of historical-positive law. Roman *aequitas,* therefore, is an application of law based on principles which, being rational and having rational human nature as a point of reference, do not transcend the juridicial phenomenon itself, but remain immanent in it (FEDELE).

Ulpian, by an application of the parameters of Stoic philosophy, defines *iurisprudentia* as

11

knowledge of things human and divine, science of the just and unjust.

Heterogeneity of Law within Sophistic Pluralism

The popularity of Sophism from the fifth century (A.D.) on demonstrates the difficulties Greek philosophy encountered as it attempted to firmly establish the unity of law ontologically, based on the central concept of nature (*physis*). Despite its internal contradictions, Sophism is based on an epistemological approach to reality, using a rational criticism like that of modern European Illuminism. Sophism developed within the cultural ethos of Athenian democracy, which embodied a great trust in reason and, consequently, in the rational and humanistic foundation of all values. Rhetoric, however — the tool of the Sophists — sacrifices universal and absolute values (FASSÒ). Rhetoric is not only the art of discussion and of persuasion used by citizens to promote the positive order of the state, but is also an instrument for the triumph of a given opinion that is made to *seem* true.

Sophism subjected not only particular laws but the entire juridical ordering of the state to rational criticism for the first time. This brought about the clamorous break between the order of nature and the juridical order of the state. A latent tension between the two orders had, of course, long existed. From this moment on, however, the juxtaposition of nature and law, of the naturally and the legally just — a juxtaposition that later found a theological analogy in Luther's theme of "Law and Gospel"—has polarized the thinking of philosophers of law.

Heraclitus, Pythagoras and traditional objectivist philosophy were all preoccupied with establishing a convergence or at least some connection between these two orders. The Sophists, however, took up the problem that had arisen in Sophocles' *Antigone*, that of the validity of positive laws that are opposed to natural or divine "unwritten" laws. In dealing with this philosophical issue, the Sophists did not limit themselves to standing the "naturally just" in opposition to the "legally just," or with proposing relativistic or natural law solutions. Occasionally, they even proposed the supremacy of human law over natural law, thus providing the basis for a first form of juridical positivism (VERDROSS).

Protagoras (d. 421 B.C.) became the teacher of a relativism founded on the principle *homo-mensural*. The human being is the measure of all values, not as an individual or as humankind, but in the sense that the opinion of the assembly of citizens, changeable over time, is considered to be the sole criterion for the validity of positive law. With no space left for a divine or a natural law, the result might have been a radical positivism, if Protagoras had not tempered his doctrine to guarantee some degree of objective unity. Thus, he considers the sense of justice common to the conscience of all people (*ethos*) as a legacy that, even if it does not allow for the formulation of univocal positive norms acceptable to all, at least allows the creation, with the help of the wiser rhetoricians, of better laws.

Sophism only occasionally produced solutions of a fully positivistic nature that declared human law and justice to be identical. Thrasymachus of Chalcedon (430–400 B.C.) was, according to Plato, among those who asserted the equivalence of law and justice. Archelaus (5–6th century B.C.), who did not belong to the Sophistic school, provided the earliest precise definition of juridicial positivism, in holding that there is no "naturally just," but only a "legally just." This definition has only been articulated in a doctrinal system in modern times.

The religious-mythological view, essentially a voluntaristic one, had sought to guarantee the unity of law by by affirming its unicity — that is, by considering law, whether divine, natural, or human, as a single global reality. Positivism has sought to affirm this unity in a more formal and extrinsic manner by affirming the unicity of *positive* law which, being founded only on the will of the human legislator, cannot escape the contradiction-riddled logic of its own internal pluralism.

A natural law current within Sophism, headed by Hippias (485–415 B.C.) opposed the relativists and the positivists. Hippias juxtaposed the precariousness of human law with the existence of "unwritten laws," and he refused to place that which is just (*dikaion*) and that which conforms to positive law (*nomimon*) on the same level. This school of thought sometimes interpreted cultural law in a naturalistic way, as when Callicles of Plato's *Gorgias* identifies the law of nature with the right of the stronger; laws that seek to limit that right, he declares, are contrary to nature and therefore unjust. At other times, though, the law of nature was interpreted rationally, as an expression of human reason. This interpretation — which represents the apex of pre-

Socratic Greek philosophy's formulation — no longer considers natural law to be an objective reality common to all beings and therefore external to humans. Rather, natural law is a norm that human beings accept because of their proper rational essence (FASSÒ).

Positive law was by now considered to be an exclusive fruit of human will. In both Hippias and Alcidamas (4th century B.C.), positive law is criticized on the basis of a tendentiously cosmopolitan natural law. This natural law's abstractness, however, frequently only reflected each philosopher's subjective ideal. Overall, Sophism failed to clarify the formal concept of law or to deduce from law any objective elements that would be valid for all. This led the Sophists to confuse natural law with an ideal and utopian one that was ultimately inadequate for establishing an ontological union between this and positive human law (VERDROSS).

Metaphysical Foundation of the Unity of Law in the Synthesis of Plato and Aristotle

These Sophists who were the contemporaries of Socrates had sought in vain to resolve the antithesis *physis/nomos*, either by establishing a mechanical relationship of dependence between the order of physical nature and the juridical, or by defining a more intrinsic but still abstract connection, as in rationalist natural law theory. Socrates (d. 399) made a leap forward by establishing a connection between morality and law. By submitting himself to the unjust sentence condemning him to death, he wished to clearly reaffirm the authority of the state, which had been undermined by the Sophists' destructive criticism. By this gesture, however, Socrates did not at all intend to assert the absolute priority of positive law, even if unjust, over natural law, nor to appeal to natural law against it. He wished simply to affirm that obedience to positive law is *not* founded on the objective and intrinsic authority that might be attributed to it through a presumed correspondence with a natural law, sophistically understood as an abstract and ahistorical reality placed above humankind.

Law is asserted to comprehend and invest the moral dimension of humankind with the duties law should inspire in a given historical situation, such as the duty of gratitude toward the Athenian state, or of solidarity because one has contractually accepted the democratic order. With Plato and Aristotle, the problem of law is definitively lifted not merely from the physical order to the rational and moral one, but also to the more properly metaphysical one (STIEGLER).

Plato (d. 347 B.C.) identifies the transcendent idea of good with being, thereby building his metaphysics. For Plato, things participate in a precarious and imperfect manner (as "traces") in the absolute being of transcendent ideas or essences. The system does not dissolve into a purely extrinsic dualism because, on the one hand, even if the form is not immanent in sensible things, there is immanence in their end (*telos*), that is, in the tension with the transcendent idea; on the other hand, because Plato, by making a voluntarist option, affirms in the *Timeus* that the Demiurge, or God, has willed that the world determined by the ideas should be as similar as possible to himself (VERDROSS). Nature is, for Plato, the true ideal and superindividual essence that transcends the sensible *physis*. The just and justice are not constituted by single historical decisions, but by the metaphysical nature of the transcendent idea of law that informs that of justice, of politics and of ethics. Thus, in the final analysis, there is only one true law because each natural and positive realization of it — even if, in order to be true, it must necessarily harken back to the transcendental idea — represents only an imitation and a trace of the archetype.

Although not a great deal of attention is given to law within Plato's philosophical system, the problem of the unity of law finds a very organic solution in it. There can be no contradiction between positive (*nomos*) and natural (*physis*) law and the transcendent idea of justice because positive law is true only insofar as it conforms to the natural law founded on the rational nature of humankind. The rational nature of humankind, on the other hand, is a reflection of the transcendent idea of justice which, in its turn, derives from the idea of the good. This fundamental position, as abstract and prevalently ethical as Socrates', explains how Plato could deduce *a priori*, by innate reminiscence of the intelligible essences, his own conception of the state, without any regard to historical experience. In the same way, he could attribute to law, not a purely juridical function, but a function of a prevalently ethical-pedagogical nature (FASSÒ).

In Plato's system, there was a risk of dissolving visible beings into an inconsistent reality. Aristotle (d. 322) overcame this problem by attributing the reality of being — known not by the Platonic reminiscence of notions already apprehended in a former life, but *a posteriori* by way of empirical experience conceptually elaborated by the intellect — not to universal and transcendent ideas (*universalia ante rem*), but to the substantial form that is immanent in each thing (*universalia in re*). It follows that single beings alone can be said to exist. The form that determines single beings and brings about their passage from potency to action is, in its immanence in them, the idea that pushes them toward their end (*entelechia*). In the achievement of this end alone do beings realize their true end, and do humans realize the morality of their existence. Beings, however, can fully realize their own proper end only by tending, at the same time, to their ultimate final cause. Although the pure act (God) is the act that properly causes, in composite beings, the passage of potency from one act to another, there is in Aristotle no concept of creation. Therefore, less coherent than Plato, he posits no origin of the ideas or forms (VERDROSS). This would eventually be done by the Judaeo-Christian concept of creation. Given that the perfect precedes the imperfect and that God, as eternal reality not composed of matter, has the fullness of being and thinks only about himself, God perceives also the forms in himself.

The problem of law is also posed in the context of this system founded on the unity of efficient and final cause (WENZEL). Justice is an essentially social virtue, based on the relation of equality or proportion *ad alterum*. Justice is no longer, as in Plato, total moral virtue and perfection of the soul. For Aristotle, the state does not constitute itself as the model of an absolute ideal of justice, but as the realization of an order that is not so much moral as juridical, that can ensure the conditions necessary for the common good. The problem, therefore, is not the ethical-pedagogical force of the law, but instead involves educating the citizen in the law on which the state founds itself (FASSÒ).

Within public law, Aristotle distinguishes between a natural and a positive law. Natural law is valid everywhere, independently of whether or not it is known, and it is deduced from rational human nature; positive law is founded on positive legislation, and its task is that of historically establishing values that, on the level of natural law, are indifferent (*bona per aliud, non bona per se*). By distinguishing between distributive and communitative justice and by further distinguishing, in his teaching on criminal liability, between error (*iuris et facti*) and ignorance, Aristotle made a great contribution to the development of juridical doctrine, even if he did not proceed to a definition of the concept of law and to the elaboration of a general theory.

It seems that Aristotle had also discerned the existence of a (divine) law of positive character for the gods (STIEGLER). In any case, he did not deal explicitly with the internal dependence and unity of this eventual trilogy, or with the traditional problem of the relationship between *physis* and *nomos*. He did, however, introduce the metaphysical premises that Scholasticism would then elaborate fully (SAUTER). In his teaching on *epikeia* (or equity), Aristotle gives an indication of the relationship between natural and positive law. Natural law, whose contents are not analytically developed by Aristotle, is the expression of our rational and essentially social human nature. Natural law, then, functions as the norm (form) for positive law which must, in turn, be intrinsically rational. In the doctrine of *epikeia*, the fundamental difference between Platonic and Aristotelian concepts of law emerges. The teacher, Plato, gives only passing attention to *epikeia*. He considers it a corruption or a merciful concession, opposed to true law, because, as a restrictive interpretation of the law, it places itself even further away from the ideal norm which is, by its very nature, general. The disciple Aristotle, however, considers it rather as a positive correction because, in creating a law historically more fitting for a specific and concrete end of the individual subject, *epikeia* realizes a truer law (HAMEL). As a consequence, *epikeia* is contradictory only in relations to the written law (WITTMANN).

Aristotle shared with Socrates a profound sense of the concrete and historical dimension of things; this led him to seek the existence of being not in Plato's transcendent ideas, but in their individual and concrete forms. This same attitude not only allowed him to leave behind the abstract and rationalistic conception of natural law that was held by the Sophists, but also led him to consider natural law a historically mutable reality rather than an absolute and fixed reality. This explains how Aristotle could accept the institution of slavery, which Stoicism alone had seriously called into question (FASSÒ).

In conclusion, it must be acknowledged that the notion of nature, polyhedric and inexhaustible in its meaning and contents, is the imperishable gift of Greek culture to the western philosophy of law. In its widest application, this notion embraces the totality of beings, from the lifeless and material to the spiritual ones, until it becomes the abstract concept of the essence of all things. Greek philosophy seized this concept and made it the foundation of a neutral natural (or divine) law — a law that exists independently of all faith in a personal being, but which is the source and origin of juridical order. This metaphysically open conception embraces the whole force of the classical idea of nature. This idea of nature overcame the crisis of Sophism — a crisis that is frequently and unjustly exaggerated (ROMMEN) — and was then mediated by Plato and Aristotle, who replaced *physis* with *metaphysis* as the foundation of juridical reality. This classical idea of nature developed, therefore, so that it was incompatible with the existence of divine law (STIEGLER). Such a law appeared in the philosophy of law with the emergence of Christian thought. This development raised again the question of the unity of law, a question the Greeks had often resolved merely formally or extrinsically, even on the level of the relationship between *physis* and *nomos* — that is, between natural and positive law.

ECLECTIC RECEPTION OF GRECO-ROMAN PHILOSOPHY BY THE CHURCH FATHERS

The Encounter of Divine Positive Law with Stoic Law

The most important contribution of Old Testament juridical thought has been the presentation of God as the immediate and personal source of law. Although the history of the Jewish people extends back over more than a millennium before the coming of Christ, the uncompromising determination and energy with which every juridical norm has constantly been referred back to Yahweh represents an extraordinary phenomenon of cultural continuity (RAPAPORT). Jewish law is never the eternal *logos*, immutable and hidden in the nature of the cosmos or in the rational nature of humankind; rather, it is a law revealed by God as his will and command, communicated to Moses and the prophets and summarized in the Decalogue.

In the Jewish conception, there is no place for the idea of a rational foundation of law (SCHÖNFELD) or consequently, for a distinction between positive and natural law. While the legalistic superimpositions of the rabbis obfuscated the essential and synthetic character of Jewish law, the intervention of the prophets further deepened its socioreligious character. By preaching holiness and the conversion of the heart, the prophets dismantled the role of exterior practice and provoked an interiorization of the ethical-juridical experience (STIEGLER). This process of interior deepening, however, eliminated all traces of natural law and accentuated the voluntaristic aspect of law even to the point of identifying the observance of the law with obedience to the will of God (FASSÒ).

The idea of divine immediacy in the establishment of law was taken up again in the New Testament; Christ, the eternal incarnate *logos*, has come to restore the original nature (or law) through the power of extending ethical-juridical norms and of rendering them binding on the new people of God (LANNE). Having received and summarized the Decalogue in the precept of the love of God and neighbor, which has continued to find expression in the Golden Rule, the New Testament allowed the question of a rational foundation for positive law to be reintroduced. The apostle Paul devalued the function of law, juxtaposed to God's justice, but did not deny the possibility of a rational knowledge of God and of natural law (FUCHS). Consequently, at the dawn of Christianity, the problem of the rational value of law, far from having been eliminated, was inserted into the great and central theological theme of the paradoxical relationship of law and grace, a theme charged with antinomian polarities. This polarity has undergone a fracture in two opposite directions, first with Pelagius and then with Luther's theme of "Law and Gospel."

With the progressive development of the constitutional and disciplinary organization of the Church (which produced its own canon law, related, as law and as institution, to the Roman one) and with the slower but irreversible affirmation of a new Christian society, the philosophical and theological confrontation with the paradoxical experience of the juridical phenomenon and with Greco-Roman culture became inevitable. There was an instinctive rejection of the earliest antinomian (Marcion), spiritualistic (Montanus) and millenaristic (Papias) movements, an innate initial hostility toward the pagan and, more importantly, the persecuting Roman state, and an awareness that Christianity held a peculiar supernatural conception of ethics. All these factors assured that the fathers of the Church, from the earliest apologists on, would exercise a most careful vigilance and criticism toward Roman jurisprudence and the philosophical-juridical culture of antiquity. This vigilant position evolved only gradually, as the Empire came under Christian influence, and only occasionally resulted in forms of naive optimism, as with Gregory the Wonderworker.

The Greek fathers were more interested in natural law theory than the Latin ones. Certain of the doctrinal safeguards guaranteed by Paul (SCHILLING), these church fathers also received — with many institutes of the *ius gentium* and *civile* — the Greek idea of a natural law dictated by reason.

Clearly, the Judeo-Christian doctrine of creation and the consequent strongly voluntaristic view of law represented both the greatest obstacle and the most effective corrective to the process of reception of rationalist natural law theory. As a result, there was a tolerance for the daring synthesis between the Judeo-sacral and the Stoic views, elaborated by Tertullian (d. after 220 A.D.), who was the first Christian author to use the concept of natural law, Origen (d. ca. 254), Lactantius (d. first half of fourth century), Clement of Alexandria (d. ca. 216–7) and John Chrysostom (d. 407). Tertullian conceived of the law promulgated by God as a positive codification of natural law; in this, he followed the example of the Hellenistic Judaism of Philo of Alexandria (d. ca. 50 A.D.) The fathers also began to distinguish between a primary natural law, valid before the Fall, and the secondary natural law that had been introduced after original sin.

The individualistic and Stoic component was corrected by the provision of a more altruistic and social dimension of natural law; the nationalistic component of the Old Testament was eliminated by acknowledging, along the lines of the Stoic model of the logos, the universal validity of ethical law (FLÜCKIGER). The early fathers, like the majority of pre-Socratic and Stoic philosophers, did not develop an organic doctrine capable of metaphysically rendering plausible their teaching on law. This also becomes clear in relation to the central problem of the unity of law. Tertullian, Origen, Cyril of Alexandria (d. 444), and Gregory of Nazianzen (d. 390) resolved this issue by a curt denial of the validity of state law that does not conform to the natural one. But the problem is posed in ethical terms (Tertullian speaks of an offense to God) rather than juridical-ontological ones.

Symptomatic of canon law's establishment as a specifically Christian juridical reality is John Chrysostom's opinion that a derogation of positive law is possible not only when the good of humanity should demand it, but also when it should be required for the good of the Church. In this way, the Church begins to be considered the criterion for evaluating positive and natural law.

The problem is taken up again by St. Ambrose (d. 397 A.D.). Although his illustrious past as a high imperial functionary had convinced him of the profound harmony between Roman and natural law, he strongly defended the priority of canon law (*censio ecclesiastica*) over imperial law (VON CAMPENHAUSEN) and, against Ulpian, he held that the prince is not *legibus solutus*. Ambrose's dependence on Seneca, from whom he borrowed the scheme of the four cardinal virtues and made it a definite part of Christian ethics, and his reliance on Cicero's *De officiis,* helped him to develop a high sense of the unity of law and morality, a unity on which he impressed a social rather than a utilitarian value.

The elaboration of a Christian natural law, refined

by contact with Stoicism, favored the insertion of the
Church into the Greco-Roman world. But it also provoked a progressive aggravation of the problem of
the compatibility of such a law with the one of grace
(divine law), whose salvific function risked being
deprived of meaning. St. Ambrose attempted to solve
this problem by positing a concordance between Law
and Grace and by holding that the extension of God's
positive law had become necessary after humankind
had abandoned the practice of natural law.

The Unity of Law in the Metaphysical and Religious Synthesis of St. Augustine

St. Augustine (d. 430 A.D.) was also influenced by
Cicero, but his views underwent other developments
as a result of contact with Pelagius (d. 427 A.D.).
From Cicero, he borrows the notion of *lex aeterna*
and, transforming it theistically, he gives this notion
the Christian feasibility that will allow it, through
the mediation of Peter Lombard (d. 1160), to become
the key concept in the medieval philosophy of law.
Breaking with Stoicism, which had identified the *lex
aeterna* with the *lex naturae* and had conceived the
latter as a substantially equal emanation of divine
reason in human reason, Augustine traces a clear
distinction between *ratio divina* and *ratio humana*.
The *lex aeterna*, as immutable as God himself, is no
longer seen as either the transcendent idea of Plato,
or Cicero's autonomously existing universal and
impersonal reason (*fatum*); rather, it is the plan for
the creation and rule of the world contained in God's
intelligence. Human reason, created by God, knows

the *lex aeterna* subjectively, *a priori*, and discovers its reflection in the *lex naturalis*, which Augustine identifies with the *ius gentium*. Natural law is no longer equal to the *lex aeterna*; it is only a trace or a rational transcription that we humans, wounded by original sin, come to know in its essential traits (*extrema lineamenta*). The eternal law becomes, therefore, the *ordo ordinans* of natural law, of the *ordo ordinatus*, specified by God first through the *lex hebraeorum* and then through the l*ex veritatis* of the New Testament, which, in its turn, is the *ordo ordinans* of the *lex temporalis* or law of the state (VERDROSS).

Within this Platonic metaphysical inspiration, but without defining further its ontological dynamic, Augustine establishes a relationship demonstrating the unity of law. In this relationship, Augustine rigorously asserts the *lex temporalis* to be subordinate to the *naturalis* and both of these in turn to the *lex aeterna*. This allows him to deny the validity of a positive law that fails to conform to natural law or to the *lex aeterna*.

While the *lex aeterna* looks toward the realization of eternal life, positive law lends itself to the creation of a worldly order. The general ethical order is, therefore, to be divided into two distinct planes that foreshadow the clear distinction that will be made by St. Thomas between the natural and the supernatural order. Morality is the vertical plane where humans move internally toward absolute duty, that is, toward the *lex aeterna*; law is the horizontal and external plane that does not generate love and whose end may also be achieved by coercion. Moreover, the state, whose function is now reduced to a purely earthly one, is not to punish all sin, but only those crimes that disturb the peaceful coexistence of human beings. By attributing a preventive purpose to penal sanctions, Augustine synthesized earlier positions that had considered them medicinal (Plato) and pedagogical (Aristotle) means, or as instruments to be used with mildness (Stoicism) (STIEGLER).

Although he distinguished law and morality with extreme clarity, Augustine caused no break between the two. Indeed, law is not merely a part of morality, but also a fulfillment of it because it renders morality binding even on the external plane (SCHILLING). What has ensued is a demythologization of the idea of the state that appeared in Greek philosophy. The state is no longer the sacral community which, by its fundamental ethical value (which Aristotle alone had rendered more specifically juridical), invests all human relations; now, the making of provisions toward the inferior spiritual and supernatural end has passed firmly to the Church (FASSÒ).

In the evolution of St. Augustine's thought, the clash with Pelagius also played a very important role. Pelagius had affirmed the goodness of human nature and the validity of salvation through good works performed in accordance with rational natural law and without the assistance of grace. Persuaded that natural law theory could lead to Pelagianism, Augustine, in opposition to his earlier views, no longer accentuates the normative nature of the *lex aeterna* understood as reason, but stresses only the binding character of God's will. This voluntaristic development is reflected when, in the *De civitate Dei*, Augustine evaluates the relative functions of the state and of the Church. At times, he seems to deny all value to the earthly city, even going so far as to call it *civitas diabuli*; at others, he grants it a certain importance, but only on' the condition that it realize Christian justice in obedience to the will of God. The Church appears at times as a mystical body and communion of saints; at others, as a visible and historical institution. From this sometimes imprecisely detailed vision (in which Luther would find ample inspiration for the doctrine of the two kingdoms and of the two churches), there emerges the tension, latent in Christian thought from the earliest times, between eschatology and history, faith and reason, grace and nature.

Augustine, while defining sin in reaction to both the external law and God's will, neither separated reason and will in God nor juxtaposed them to each other. This explains how he could influence in equal measure both the intellectualistic and the voluntaristic schools in the Middle Ages.

SUPERIMPOSITION OF DIVINE AND NATURAL LAW FROM LATE ANTIQUITY TO SCHOLASTICISM

The end of classical antiquity and the beginning of the early Middle Ages were profoundly marked by three events. First, the collection of the Eastern conciliar canons and the papal decretals of the fifth century (384–498) were translated into Latin, meriting Dyonisius Exiguus (d. ca. 550) the title "father of canon law." Second, the great eclectic compendium of past Christian juridical doctrine, compiled by Isidore of Seville (d. 636), was published in the

Etymologiae. Here, in addition to the views of the church fathers, those of the Roman juriconsults were also fully elaborated for the first time. And finally, this era was marked by the encounter of Christian thought with the spirit of Germanic law.

Among the fundamental attributes of Germanic law to first stand out was the strong religious and sacred component that emerged in such institutes as the trial by ordeal (judgment of God) or of the *treuga Dei*, but especially in the *leges barbarorum*, in which the law's dependence on God is programmatically declared. Other basic traits of Germanic law included the priority assigned to custom over written law; the concrete character of law, no longer considered abstractly, as by the Romans, but as an attribute of things and persons; a popular component — on the strength of which the prince is no longer considered to be, like the Roman emperor, *legibus solutus* — making law national, but also potentially cosmopolitan, demonstrating the fact that feudal society was structured along a horizontal and not a vertical hierarchy. These attributes were easily integrated by, and provoked further developments in, Christian juridical thought, a thought based on the divine immediacy and unity of law, on the strong theological value of tradition and on the contemporaneously universal and particular structure of the Church.

Isidore of Seville (560–636 A.D.), taking up again an idea of St. Augustine's, had already expressly underlined the customary and dynamic element of Germanic law. This was later done also by Gratian (d. ca. 1142) and Sicardus of Cremona (d. 1216). Isidore held that the dependence of positive law on natural law could not be declared abstractly and, in deriving positive law from natural law, one had to consider the exigencies and customs of each group and each nation. However, the fact that the equivocal naturalistic and Stoic-Ulpianean conception of natural law as natural instinct did endure from the early Middle Ages to the time of the Scholastics was not unrelated to the material concreteness of Germanic law. On this point also, Isidore made a step forward by omitting the reference to animals from the Ulpianean definition of natural law. Perhaps unwittingly, Isidore thereby allowed for the beginning of a process of refining the naturalistic conception of natural law. This conception, with its pantheistic overtones, had presented one of the more difficult obstacles to the acceptance of the Greek physis in Christian thought. Stephen of Tournai (d. 1203), six centuries later, would eliminate all possibility of misunderstanding by firmly denying the juridical competency of animals.

There was even greater historical significance in the fact that Isidore of Seville, following the religious-sacral line of the fathers (FASSÒ) — who had not succeeded in producing a clear distinction between philosophy and theology — once again identified natural with divine law. This same superimposition would surprisingly allow Gratian to continue defining the *ius naturale* as that law "q*uod in lege et evangelio continetur*" [that is contained in the law and the gospel] (WENGER). Beginning with this premise, it was inevitable that, even at the level of ethics and law, Gratian should develop a sacral and voluntaristic option, thus affirming in another *dictum* that, in natural law, "*nihil aliud praecipatur, quam quod Deus vult fieri, nihilque vetitur, quam quod Deus* *prohibet fieri"* [nothing whatsoever must be commanded except what God wills, and nothing must be forbidden except what God prohibits] (D. 9 c. 11). At the same time, and adhering to Augustinian tradition, Gratian also furthered the phenomenon of the interiorization of law, both by more clearly defining the distinction between sin and crime (defined no longer in relation to social disorder, but by reference to the scandal caused within the Church) and by establishing the principle, *nulla poena sine culpa,* as a fundamental development of penal canon law. By holding, moreover, that coercion is not essential to the notion of law, Gratian contributed to the permanent embedding of this doctrine in Christian juridical thought (STIEGLER).

The preoccupation with guaranteeing the unity of law grew steadily throughout the Middle Ages. This happened because the prominent authors — even when, with varying degrees of awareness, they offered divergent fundamental options, both intellectualistic and voluntaristic — did not deny the possibility of the coexistence of divine and natural law. Moreover, they repeatedly affirmed the invalidity of positive laws that were opposed to natural law, such laws being defined as *vana et irrita* by Gratian, and the impossibility of dispensing positive law from the precepts of natural law, as was held, for example, by Huguccio (d. 1210).

There was also a great attempt by St. Anselm (d. 1109), Hugh of St. Victor (d. 1141), Alexander of Hales (d. 1245) and others, to synthesize natural law, along the lines of the most authentic biblical tradition, around a single supreme principle from which ever less general norms could be progressively derived

(WOLF). Within the context of a hierarchically organized feudal structure, this movement evidently stimulated the effort already begun by the fathers to define natural law according to a hierarchical order. Thus, William of Auxerre (d. 1231–1237) distinguished among a *ius naturale generalissimum, generalius et speciale,* while St. Bonaventure (d. 1274) affirmed the existence of absolutely valid principles and principles valid for the economy of salvation and, therefore, necessary only before and after the Fall. This speculative effort toward a *reductio ad unum,* based on an even more precise set of values (FLÜCKIGER), was contemporaneous with the dawning awareness of the political and religious unity of the *sacrum romanum imperium.* As a juridical consequence, the theory — in the formula attributed to Irnerius (twelfth century), of the *unum esse ius, cum unum sit imperium* — of the necessity of a single common law, valid for all nations, emerged. Indeed, the juridical unity of Christendom was achieved when, after long discussion, canon law was accepted, with Justinian's Roman law, as universally valid. The formula of the *utrumque ius* expressed the conviction that a two-pronged but single law existed, universally valid and founded in divine law (FASSÒ).

In any case, the impossibility of achieving a perfect synthesis centered around the Golden Rule, if not, as was attempted by Simon of Bisignano (d. early thirteenth century), around the theological concept of *caritas.* Undoubtedly, this lack of synthesis also involved the inability of the pre-Scholastics to produce a unitary definition of natural law and to distinguish it from the *ius divinum positivum,* the latter being first so named by Abelard (d. 1142).

Indeed, pre-Scholastic theologians and canonists continued to include in their works, as in the *Decretum*, all the conceptions of natural law elaborated by the Greeks and transmitted by the fathers. Frequently, these writers were aware of the reciprocal incongruence of the sacral (identifying natural law with divine law), the naturalistic (identifying it with natural instinct) and the rationalistic (defining it as a law dictated by human reason) conceptions of natural law.

With the success of Aristotelianism through the work of St. Albert the Great (d. 1280), it became possible to elaborate a clearer distinction not only between reason and faith and philosophy and theology, but also between natural and divine positive law. This was, after all, a distinction already propounded by Ruphinus (d. 1192) a century earlier. The task of assigning their own academic categorizations to the various concepts of law was performed by St. Albert himself. Natural law in its Platonic form, conceived of as "natural justice" (that is, as a cosmic natural justice), because of its ethical importance, was placed under the heading of metaphysics or the science of nature. The naturalistic Stoic-Ulpianean view, transmitted by Isidore of Seville and Gratian, was eliminated because it was incompatible with the exclusively anthropological character of law. The rationalistic concept, understood as a norm dictated by reason and held by Albert to be the only true form of natural law, was assigned to philosophy. Finally, the *ius divinum positivum*, also issuing from the tradition of Isidore and Gratian, was attributed to theology (FASSÒ).

The problem of the relationship between and the unity of natural and divine law would find an ontologically plausible solution only in St. Thomas Aquinas (d. 1274). By producing a synthesis of the Aristotelian empirical-conceptual method with the theological and Platonistic one of Augustine. Thomas merited not only the title of *doctor angelicus,* but also that of *doctor communis* (VERDROSS).

THE UNITY OF LAW IN THE DISTINCTION BETWEEN NATURAL AND SUPERNATURAL IN ST. THOMAS

St. Thomas takes from Aristotle the ilemorphistic system and emphasizes the final cause. The entelechy intrinsic to the nature of things is the principle that dominates the structure of beings (VERDROSS). This ontological tension, which drives the imperfect being toward its metaphysical perfection, becomes the foundation of ethics. Human beings can fully realize their ethical-metaphysical identities only by reaching their final end, God, who has created humankind in his own image and likeness. In St. Thomas, Aristotelian teleology becomes transcendence.

From Cicero and St. Augustine, on the other hand, St. Thomas receives the idea of the *lex aeterna*, which coincides with the rational plan God uses to lead the world toward its final end. Human beings know the *lex aeterna* only mediately, through the ontological irradiation of it that they find in their own rational nature.

In interpreting the fundamental inclinations of our own rational human nature — which we must evaluate by using the principle of equality and proportion, but also by taking into account contingent historical circumstances — we formulate dynamically the norms of natural law. Thomas, in the wake of the preceding tradition, also elaborated a supreme and synthetic principle of natural law and identified it with the twofold duty of love of God and of neighbor (which logically precedes that of the Golden Rule). From this, then, must be derived the other norms which, after all, are already presupposed or contained, explicitly or implicitly, in the Decalogue.

From natural law, to which Thomas at times assigns also the *ius gentium*, is derived human law, *per modum conclusionis* and *determinationis* or, in the case of indifferent values, *per modum additionis*. Human law, therefore, does not issue from the nature of things with the same "mechanicity" as natural law; it arises from common agreement or from the (reasonable) command of the prince. The conclusion remained that a human law opposed to the natural one, aside from lacking an ethically binding force, could not exist as law at all, at least in logic; such human law is a *corruptio legis* that places itself outside the juridical sphere.

St. Thomas, indulging in a certain intellectual optimism, assigns to reason a primacy over the will, because the activity of the will presupposes that of reason. However, in holding that the will is necessary for the promulgation of the law, defined as *ordinatio rationis*, Thomas assigns to the will a primacy of its own in relation to the freedom of human action (MANSER), so avoiding in some measure a rigid intellectualism. The ontological presupposition of this equilibrium is the identity in God between will and reason; because of this identity, God can only will that which is rational. At the human level, where will and reason are two different faculties, unity is guaranteed by the fact that right practical reason, which is precisely that by which humans participate in the divine essence, cannot propose to the will a law other than that dictated by divine reason itself.

The undeniable rationalistic inclination of St. Thomas also emerges from the prevalently metaphysical approach he uses to discuss the *lex aeterna*, as if it, like the natural law, were placed over the world only to direct it toward its natural end. In truth, even if Thomas does not establish an explicit hierarchical relationship between *lex aeterna* and *ius divinum* (distinguished in *ius naturale* and *ius divinum positivum*) — as will be done three and a half centuries later by Suárez — he is certainly aware that the *lex divina*, like the *lex naturalis*, consists merely in participation, if of a higher type in the *lex aeterna*: *"lex divinitus data, per quam lex aeterna participatur altiori modo"* [the divine law, through which the eternal law participates in a fuller way] (I–II, q.91 a.5).

Next to the metaphysical unity of the trilogy *lex aeterna / naturalis / humana* resulting from the symbiosis of the ilemorphistic system and theonomic Christian one, Thomas places the theological unity that exists between *lex aeterna* and *lex divina (positiva)*. This is revealed by God not only to guide us toward our supernatural end, but also to provide for the imperfections of human laws. The ontological relationship between *lex aeterna* and *lex divina* results from Thomas's theological system, which is founded on the affirmation of the connaturality of reason and faith and of the superiority of faith over reason. This is expressed by the principle, *"gratia perficit, non destruit, naturam.*" Reason is called to prepare the *preambula* of faith and to explain its truths. In its negative form, this relationship of unity is defined by St. Thomas's emphatic affirmation that a human law contrary to the divine one, *nullo modo licet observare.*

By distinguishing courageously between the natural and the supernatural planes, Thomas resolved the doubt raised by the fathers concerning the compatibility of natural law with the divine (positive) one. In addition, he also definitively eliminated the possible pantheistic elements concealed in identifying natural with divine law, as had been done by Isidore of Seville and Gratian. By making this distinction, St. Thomas preserved both the rationalistic element of Stoic natural law theory and the religious and sacral one of the Judeo-Christian tradition (FASSÒ). It ought not to be forgotten, however, that this religious element had already been received in the Patristic and Scholastic concept of *lex aeterna*, which implies the affirmation of God's role as immediate and personal source of law. Thomas reached the apex of the Scholastic reflection on law and formulated a series of important conclusions (SCHÖNFELD). He distinguished between law — whose intersubjective dimension regulates the exterior actions of humans — and morality, while reaffirming in any case their fundamental unity because of the principle that human laws also bind in the *forum conscientiae*. Thomas held that coercion was not an essential element in the notion of law, but only a moment of conditional necessity. He differentiated between objective and subjective law, between *subiectum* (the human alone) and *obiectum* (always other than the human), *titulus* and *terminus iuris (*point of reference for legal obligation). As a consequence, St. Thomas recognized sociality, equality (which distinguishes itself in distributive, commutative and legal justice) and necessity as features of law.

DIVINE WILL AS THE SOLE SOURCE OF THE UNITY OF LAW IN OCKHAMISM

The equilibrium established by St. Thomas between reason and will was broken almost immediately by the radicalization of voluntaristic theses. The question, for example, was asked: Is the juridical order an immutable realization of the *lex aeterna* existing in God's intellect, or is it the mutable result of the positive command of his will, not bound to the *ratio divina*? While rationalism places God's freedom in jeopardy, voluntarism runs the risk of denying the intrinsic reality of things (STIEGLER).

Voluntarism has its philosophical roots in the nominalism of Boetius (d. 524 A.D.) who, in the application of a rigid realism of neo-Platonic origin, had denied all real content to Aristotelian categories. The *universalia*, which later became a major concern of the Middle Ages, are only *nomina* — that is, conventional and abstract notions of the intellect, empty of real content. Individual beings alone (*universalia post rem*) really exist. Metaphysics is replaced by a system in which the essence of things is established in each case by God's will. Thus, God does not will something because it is good, but something is good because it is willed by God: *quod Deus vult, hoc est iustum!* The Aristotelian-Thomistic *telos*, intrinsically placed by God in created things (*entelechia*) yields its place to an extrinsic finality. As a consequence, ethics are also no longer founded in metaphysics, but in obedience to the will of God.

Voluntaristic nominalism arose in reaction to the potentially impersonal and neutral character of the Stoic-rationalist natural law theory that had occasionally affected certain branches of Scholasticism. Nominalism not only rediscovered, in all its power, the biblical idea of the immediacy of God in the production of law, but it also had the distinction of orienting theological research toward the empirical analysis of nature, so creating the cultural prerequisites for the birth of modern experimental science. Medieval objectivism was replaced by a subjectivism that conferred a more existential dimension on ethics and allowed for a more circumstantiated evaluation of the specific individual and of history.

The grafting of the Franciscan religious voluntarism of Augustinian inspiration onto the nominalist tradition through Roscellinus of Compiegne (d. 1120–1125), Abelard (d. 1142), St. Bonaventure (d. 1274) and Roger Bacon (d. ca. 1292) received its first systematic elaboration in the work of John Duns Scotus (d. 1308). In opposition to St. Thomas, who had defined as a fictitious abstraction the possibility that God, *de potentia absoluta*, might act against the order of his own wisdom, Duns Scotus held that God does not act *de potentia ordinata* because he is not subject to any law and, therefore, not even to the *lex aeterna*. Given that the *voluntas* is superior to the *ratio,* God wills that which he wills without any other motive than his own will, whose formal limits are set only by the principle of contradiction.

The central category of the system of the *doctor*

subtilis is not reason, as for Thomas, but love. The metaphysical-religious nature of this polyhedrous category saved Duns Scotus from falling into a radical positivism. Love, which resides in God's will, is the superior ethical principle. However, love manifests itself at the level of natural law, in an abstract sense, only in the first two precepts of the Decalogue: the love of God and the love of neighbor. God, who may change all other social norms, cannot dispense with the observance of these precepts. Moreover, these two commandments seem to find their foundation not in reason, but in the obligation to obey God's will. Duns Scotus saved *in extremis* the existence of natural law and the unity of law through the principle that human norms, in order to be valid, must be *consona primis principiis* — that is, consonant with God's love. However, the *doctor subtilis* came close to assuming a positivist position with the thesis that obedience to an unjust human law takes priority over the obligation to follow one's own erroneous conscience.

Nominalist empiricism acquired greater rigidity with William of Ockham (d. 1349). The instrument of knowledge is no longer, as in Thomism, the capacity of reason for abstraction, but empirical experience (GRABMANN); God and supernatural truths, not being subject to philosophical investigation, can be accepted by *homo in via* only through faith. They can be known truly only in the beatific vision, that is, by *homo in patria*. *Recta ratio* is no longer the autonomous instrument by which humans, knowing the essences of things, come to know God, but the instrument through which God makes his will known to humans. Reason, then, is essentially left with the task of rendering plausible the fact that it is

41

necessary to obey the absolutely free and arbitrary will of God (FASSÒ). Morality now resides exclusively in obeying God's will.

In the more polemical expressions of his thought (KÖLMEL), it appears that Ockham eliminated even the last remains of a rational natural law. Thus, in relation to Duns Scotus, the *venerabilis inceptor* takes a radical step forward by holding that even the first two precepts of the Decalogue have a contingent and positive character. If there were no logical contradiction, God could also command that he should be hated (VERDROSS). Natural law, whether explicitly or implicitly, is wholly contained in Scripture and, therefore, can no longer be distinguished from divine law. *All* law, insofar as it finds its ultimate source in the will of God, may be called divine law.

Nevertheless, Ockham is as emphatic as all medieval authors in affirming the nullity of human laws, whether civil or canonical, that do not conform both to divine law and to an "open" reason (*ratio aperta* or *recta*). By this latter requirement, Ockham demonstrated that he could not free himself wholly from the Thomistic tradition (OTT). Apart from this affirmation, Ockham preserved the unity of law not so much by establishing an intrinsic metaphysical relationship among divine, natural and human law, but by shifting the problem onto the unicity of law. Divine law, in his scheme, makes all things the expression of God's will.

Although Ockham affirms nominalistically and conceptually that there is no ontological connection between immanence and transcendence, between the world and God (where the relationship is not established by reason, but by faith), he did not go so far (as Luther would two centuries later) as to intrinsically separate human law from the divine one. Ockham's political views notwithstanding, he was not able to separate himself totally from the cultural environment of the later Middle Ages and to entirely abandon the Thomistic doctrine of the *natura non deleta*; as a consequence, despite his mistrust of metaphysics, he is compelled to preserve, at least formally, an intrinsic relationship between transcendence and the world.

It was inevitable that the imbalance caused by the voluntaristic rigidity of the viscerally antimetaphysical *via moderna* should trespass from the philosophical into the theological sphere. Gabriel Biel (1420–1495), a pure voluntarist in ethics but an intellectualist as to the foundation of natural law, completed the process with regard to soteriology a century and a half after Ockham. In this, Biel was a forerunner of Martin Luther (1483–1546), over whom, in fact, he was to have great influence (OTT). If sin cannot be qualified as such because of the intrinsic immorality of the action, then justification cannot be the reward for any human merit, but only a nonimputation of fault by God. The Protestant doctrine of predestination, already anticipated by Wycliff (d. 1384), was to be the extreme consequence of this radical Ockhamism (ROMMEN).

RATIONALITY AS ULTIMATE SOURCE OF LAW IN INTELLECTUALISM

Gregory of Rimini (d. 1358) made an attempt to reestablish a balance between will and reason by introducing some rationalist elements of the *via antiqua* into voluntarism. This attempt led, in turn, to an intellectualist response.

By distinguishing between the *lex indicativa*, which points out good and evil, and the *lex imperitiva*, which commands the performance of good and the avoidance of evil, Gregory of Rimini reached the conclusion that sin is already committed when the *lex indicativa* is violated, even before God intervenes with the command of his *lex imperitiva*. Moreover, Ockham's disciple held that the violation of a *recta aliqua ratio*, whether angelic or human, constitutes a sin, even if, *"per impossibile ratio divina sive Deus ipse non esset"* [through an absurdity divine mind or God himself did not exist] (*Sent.* I d. 34 a.2). This hypothesis became famous later, not only because it was received by Biel and, three centuries later, by Hugo Grotius (d. 1645), the founder of modern rationalist natural law theory, but because, above all, already in the late Middle Ages this did not seem to be blasphemous. For ethics (or, if one prefers, natural law), in the late Middle Ages begins that process of secularization that is completed only by modern rationalism or juridical positivism, with the definitive elimination of God as the immediate source of natural law.

A further progression was achieved by Gabriel Vásquez (d. 1601), who separated reason as a subjective element from the rational human nature. Vásquez held that the ultimate criterion of morality is not reason as Thomistically understood because it is too easily subject to error; rather, morality is defined by the rational nature of human beings as an objective reality. Consequently, only that which corresponds with rational human nature is moral and just.

Any return to the rationalistic views of Greco-

Roman philosophy was now being impeded both by the biblical doctrine of the immediacy of God in the production of law and by the Patristic and Thomistic teachings on the unity of law. In this context, Vásquez, a strong supporter of the notion of *natura pura* in theology, distinguished between a *lex naturalis primaria*, furnished by the rational nature of human beings, and a *lex naturalis secondaria*, furnished by reason. On the basis of this distinction, Vásquez held that primary natural law and the essences of things, even if they have their origins in God, are preordained by his *ratio*. Thus, things exist as autonomous realities, independently of whether or not God wills and knows them. God's freedom consists only in the fact that he may decide whether or not to create them; if he chooses to create them, God must respect their already preconstituted model. The unity of law is no longer guaranteed, as in Thomism, by the fact that primary natural law, or rational human nature, exists in an ontological participation in the *lex aeterna,* but by the fact that the divine Spirit directly illuminates the judgment of the human intellect, that is, the secondary natural law. As Biel had suggested, the immediacy of God in the production of law and in the unity of law are no longer bound together directly, in the intrinsic relationship existing between *lex aeterna* and *lex naturalis*, but only indirectly, through the divine illumination of human reason.

The final logical conclusions of this intellectualism limiting God's freedom were also formulated in Spain by the jurist Fernandus Vazquez de Menchaca (d. 1589). His thesis held that reason and natural law coincide so that the second is the self-sufficient product of the first.

Thus, at the end of the Middle Ages, in a repetition of the experience of the Stoic-Ciceronian model, law was separated from metaphysics. This left the field ready for Hugo Grotius (1583–1645), who would find much inspiration in the Thomism mediated by Spanish moral theology, a theology that tended to humanistically deepen the anthropological subjective dimension of ethics. This theology was also marked, however, by a strong theological conception of the extrinsic relationship between nature and grace. Grotius would provide the basis for the new natural law, different from the Scholastic conception because it is no longer considered a fruit of the ontological participation of rational human nature in the *lex aeterna*. Instead, natural law is the exclusive product of a human reason that is not connected to the intellect or will of God, or even to his very existence, and not bound, therefore, by any supernatural or theological presupposition (FASSÒ).

The transition from philosophical intellectualism to soteriological theology was also initiated by Biel. Given that the divine promulgation of a law does no more than confirm that which we humans already know through our *scintilla conscientiae* or *sinderesis,* the Decalogue, which is binding because of its intrinsic rationality, is materially natural law while being divine positive law only in a formal sense (OTT). Therefore, even the law of the Old Testament — and, ultimately, the entire *ius divinum positivum* — becomes binding only subjectively (*interius in corde*), as corresponding (*consonans*) to the exigencies of natural law or to rational human nature.

By combining a radical voluntarism (a consequence of the doctrine that had already emerged in

Ockhamism of the *natura totaliter deleta*, which eliminates all possibility of a rational natural law) with the subjectivism that had emerged in the intellectualism of Gabriel Biel, Martin Luther would radicalize the problem. Revelation as such — that is, the *lex Dei* or *Christi* or *ius divinum* — is a Word pronounced by God no longer *ad nos*, with a formal and objective binding force (as Catholic theology would continue to hold); it is, rather, a *Verbum Dei in nos*, whose binding force depends on the way in which the individual accepts it in faith, *interius in corde*.

With the axioms *sola fide*, *sola gratia* and *sola scriptura,* a truly radical religious voluntarism begins (ROMMEN). Having broken the intrinsic ontological relationship between faith and reason, between the natural and the supernatural, the philosophy of law becomes incapable of finding a role as *ancilla* in the mystery of salvation. From the Renaissance and the Reformation onward, the philosophy of law has continued to develop, but it has been sustained by reason alone and, therefore, it has recidivously issued into juridical positivism.

By separating, on the theological level, divine from human law and rendering impossible an incarnation of divine law in the human, Luther exacerbated the antinomy between faith and reason, the invisible and the visible Church, law and love. This allowed Christian thought to face the problem of law no longer in a philosophical-theological context, but in an exclusively theological one. Luther unconsciously created the preconditions for a theology of law that would also become a theology of canon law; this development would first take place in

Protestantism and then, after Rudolph Sohm's (d. 1917) failure to create an irremediable antinomy between Church and law, in the Catholic sphere.

THE SYNTHESIS OF CHRISTIAN THOUGHT AROUND THE SUAREZIAN FORMULA: "JUS DIVINUM, SIVE NATURALE, SIVE POSITIVUM"

When Franciscus Suárez (1548–1617) produced a synthesis of Christian juridical thought in his powerful *Tractatus de Legibus ac Deo Legislatore* (1612), Gabriel Vásquez had already declared the immenence of ethics in a human nature identified with reason, and Martin Luther had already denied the soteriological character of the visible Church, so rendering divine and human law incompatible with each other. The preoccupation with correcting the intellectualistic rationalism of Vázquez and with controversially opposing the spirit of Luther's thought allowed Suárez to elaborate a synthesis of Thomism and Ockhamism.

Suárez continued to enjoy the illusion, which the Peace of Augsburg (1555) had not yet dispelled, of a political-religious unity of Christendom. He also accepted the idea of the global dependence of all things on the will of God and, therefore, tendentially also from the *ius divinum*, an idea advanced by Ockhamism and strengthened by the doctrine of the Reformers. These factors led Suárez to build his system around a verticalism whose nature is theological and moral rather than philosophical.

At the centre of the new synthesis, as in Thomism, is the *lex aeterna,* which is identified with God and regulates all his works *ad extra*. Although the *lex aeterna* is *ut sic obligativa* — that is, sufficient to bind — it binds *exterius* only when it is promulgated by another law. The law that promulgates it *ad extra* and from which it is, therefore, formally distinct, is the *ius divinum;* from the *ius divinum* derive, as participation at the natural and supernatural levels (*participatio excellentior*), the *ius naturale* and the *ius divinum positivum*. The Suarezian triad — *ius divinum*, s*ive naturale*, s*ive positivum* — replaces the Thomistic one and becomes the common patrimony of Catholic theology and of canon law, as it was received in the former *Codex Iuris Canonici* (cc. 27. 2 and 1509).

The priority of the supernatural end over the natural one, already affirmed by St. Thomas, is spontaneously translated by Suárez on the institutional level, conforming to the spirit of his times. If the state has the function of educating good citizens, the Church, which enjoys an indirect power over the State, has the function of rendering people good.

At the level of an analysis that is more metaphysical than political or institutional, Suárez succeeds in maintaining a great equilibrium between voluntarism and intellectualism. Law is now considered as the joint result of intellect and will, which in God are an *actus simplex*. Consequently, the *doctor eximius* affirms, against Gregory of Rimini, that natural law is not only *indicativa boni et mali*, but also *imperativa*. Human reason, indeed, can conceive God only as he who binds us to the observance of that which is dictated by his own divine reason (*De legibus*, II, 6 and I, 5). Around this point, Suárez synthesizes with deep logical unity the traditional doctrine that had already surfaced in the thinking of the church fathers. Given that natural law contains a real element of obligation, it is binding even before it is promulgated by a human law and, therefore, renders any contrary positive norm invalid and never allows for dispensation. In opposition to Vázquez, Suárez reaffirms a more Thomistic metaphysical position; he denies that natural law can be the exclusive and autonomous expression of rational human nature regarded separately from human reason or as a secondary natural law. For Suárez, the ontological connection with the *lex aeterna* is not guaranteed indirectly through the divine illumination of the human intellect, but directly, because otherwise natural law would not exist, *si Deus non daretur*.

Reason is merely the organ of our rational human nature; it has the function of discovering the fundamental principles of natural law in this nature. Natural law is understood in such a way that it also includes all logically necessary conclusions. In the footsteps of St. Augustine, St. Thomas, and the Spanish moral theologians of his times, Suárez, with a profound sense of individual reality, avoided all abstractions (FASSÒ). He formulated the teaching that would become classic in later Catholic thought on both the problem of the intrinsic unity of natural law and on the question of the absolute validity of this same law. Law divides itself into three groups of norms: the general ones (*honestum est faciendum*), the more particular ones (*Deus est colendus*) and those that are more difficult to apprehend (condemnation of adultery). While stressing firmly the immutability, universality and unbreakability of natural law, Suárez affirmed that, depending on the human circumstances in which natural law is to be applied, the first principles remain the same but may command different things.

With St. Thomas, the *bonum commune* had become the fundamental criterion of natural law. In response to St. Augustine, who had Platonistically believed that in God there exist *plures rationes rerum,* Thomas had held that the *lex aeterna* is unique because the *bonum commune*, of which this law is the *ratio,* is unique and all things are to be ordered for this common good. Suárez develops this concept as he analyzes it in greater depth. On the one hand, he holds that the *bonum commune* does not include the *bonum communitatis* alone, but also the *felicitas singulorum* and, correspondingly, that the *felicitas singulorum* is not conceivable except in relation to the *bonum communitatis.* On the other hand, he asserts that there is not only a *bonum commune*, but also a *bonum commune omnium nationum.*

Thus, Suárez takes up again and develops the questions that had been posed to Christian juridical thought by the discovery of the New World and by the Protestant Reformation. These questions regarding natural law had first been faced by Franciscus de Vitoria (d. 1546) who, by transforming the *ius gentium* into a *ius inter gentes*, had become the father of modern international law (VERDROSS). Suárez holds that the nations of the world represent not only a physical unity, but also a moral and political one; therefore, they require a single juridical order. It seems, however, that the theologian from Coimbra who, with great perspicacity, foretells the constitution of an international body endowed with coercive power intends to base international law on the

51

customary law created by the several states rather than on natural law as de Vitoria did (FASSÒ).

Suárez was profoundly at ease in the culture of his times, both in its developments of the modern concept of an absolutist territorial state and in its expression of an ecclesiology oriented toward institutional problems. As a consequence, Suárez places great importance on the role of the human legislator, whether secular or ecclesiastical, in the process of the production of law (STIEGLER). In this same area, however, he follows preceding Christian thought while, at the same time, his tendency toward voluntarism is allowed to surface. This voluntarism is encouraged at the philosophical level by the fact that, while in God the unity between reason and will is perfect and constitutes a simple act, in humans the same unity is complex because we can only proceed *cum successione et discursu* [step by step and by making distinction].

In contrast with the teaching of the *Defensor Pacis* regarding the indirect divine origin of state power, Suárez holds that the human legislator, still considered as *minister Dei,* receives the power to govern the state, insofar as it is a *societas perfecta,* directly from God. Suárez, therefore, in line with the most authentic Christian tradition, not only considers the prince as *legibus solutus,* but also attributes to him the power to bind his subjects in conscience. Moreover, following Castro (d. 1558) and Medina (d. 1578), Suárez attributes to the prince the power of deriving from his own intention even the nature (*sub gravi or sub levi*) of the obligation imposed by the law, or the nonbinding nature of the same in conscience (*leges mere peonales*).

Suárez follows this biblical Christian interiorization of law, but not without superimposing the moral plane on the juridical one. He introduces the *exceptio a voluntate principis*, of clear Platonic and voluntaristic inspiration, as a third case of *epikeia* along with the first two, objective in nature, elaborated by Aristotle and St. Thomas and based on the *exceptio a potestate* (HAMEL).

In opposition to Marsilius of Padua (d. 1342–43), Jan Hus (d. 1415) and to the Protestant reformers, Suárez sought to provide a theoretical framework for both secular and ecclesiastical power. His theological argumentation found an *a posteriori* guarantee in Scripture rather than a *locus theologicus* capable of generating an original ecclesiological system. It was inevitable, therefore, that the difference between the secular and the ecclesiastical legislator should be summarized in the principle that the Church alone has the power to exact from its members the performance of interior acts. This principle was eventually received in the former *Codex Iuris Canonici*.

Christian juridical thought had always faced the problem of secular and canon law by using the same formal concept of law and by applying the same methodological process. With Suárez, this process reached the apex of its development. Medieval theologians and canonists had developed a formal concept of law based on a substantially philosophical ontology and gnosiology. When discussed theologically, the corrective criterion of an "elevation" to the supernatural was applied to this concept of law. Through Suárez's mediation, this became the view of law underlying the entire juridical system of the former *Codex Iuris Canonici*. This concept had undergone no substantial modifications since Tridentine times, although neo-Scholasticism attempted to reintroduce it in a new dress, more consonant with the requirements of modern thought. The magisterium of the Church made ample use of it in the *Syllabus* and in the social encyclicals, in the frequently polemical attempt to dialogue with the modern currents in the philosophy of law (STIEGLER).

Given the more or less explicit premise, at work from the early Middle ages on, that canon law is valid not only for the Church but also for Christendom, the awareness that a theological doctrine of canon law needs to be developed — free from the preoccupation of being, at the same time, a philosophy (or, eventually, a theology) valid also for secular law — has been able to emerge only in the last 25 years. This awareness was stimulated by Protestant theology and the openness to pluralism brought about by Vatican II.

3

The Unity of Law in Orthodox, Protestant and Catholic Theology

THE CULTURAL BACKGROUND

The specific and divergent responses of Orthodox, Protestant and Catholic theologies regarding the nature of canon law may be gathered only when we consider the fundamental cultural options in which these theologies become historically embedded even as they preserve, in diverse ways, the substance of a Christian discourse. As human beings, we always begin from these cultural options when we seek to interpret the world, searching for the truth about ourselves and the meaning of our own history.

Humankind is forever attempting to evade "the

diabolical circle of cosmic appearances" without resting within it, "like the serpent which bites its own tail" (VON BALTHASAR). This attempt has constantly resulted in two solutions which, despite the variety of specific forms and contents, are in some way continuously recurring. The first is the Eastern way, which, faced with the absolute nature of being, accepts the absolute relativity of history. This leads to an attempt to escape from the contingent nature of history, in order to return to the original purity of the "divine." Here, the divine is conceived as an indistinct, homogeneous and infinite reality that transcends all that is human. This philosophical elevation, perpendicular to the horizontal direction of history, allows a Platonistic overcoming of earthly contradiction. In living a history-less eschatology, however, this way of thinking ultimately betrays our human destiny to make the world our own (EVDOKIMOV).

The second way, the Western one, bases itself on our human desire to gather the ultimate destiny of ourselves and of reality from the concreteness of our own history. This way of thinking tends to identify God with history, which is understood as a plan that we humans realize and in which we live without eschatological perspective. First reflected in Judaic Messianism, this view was taken up in the West by Karl Marx (1818–1883) who, by putting forth the idea of progress, gave form to the most conscious and shrewd expression of the Promethean myth. Positivist determinism, on the basis of historical dialectic, has produced only a pitiless forward pushing pragmatism. This pragmatism is barely overcome by the principle of *hope* advanced by E. Bloch which, however, ultimately refers back to eschatology and prophecy (VON BALTHASAR).

Christianity, because of its incarnational principle, precludes all possibility of escape from the world, whether toward the heights or by great leaps forward. Christians are called to take up the mandate for the world without surrendering to the temptation of achieving salvation by purely human means; the only salvation meaningful to them is that of God made flesh. They cannot offer consolation to anyone by reference to the contemplation of some Platonic archetype or by the promise of a perfect tomorrow. Christians know that they must begin to change the world immediately, by welcoming grace as a force that surpasses their own strength and with a hope that stands against all the hopes of our time because it is grounded in the resurrection of Christ and of all those who have died.

The incarnational principle, however, comes to be interpreted with all the rigor of the Catholic tradition. In metaphysics, Catholic theology receives the ilemorphistic Aristotelian and Thomistic view summarized in the principle *"universalia in rebus,"* as opposed to the *"universalia ante res"* (Platonism) or to the *universalia post res* (nominalism). According to this principle, form becomes *incarnated* in matter; on this basis, with extreme doctrinal coherence and without any break in methodological continuity, Catholic theology makes the passage both from Chalcedonian Christology — common to all the great Christian confessions — to the Church as institution, and from the justifying and uncreated grace of God to sanctifying and created grace. On the strength of this view — which reflects the Latin cultural values of concreteness and balance — Christians are immediately bound to cooperate in a work of salvation "in" and "of" this world. They live eschatology in the historical present even as they are aware of the impossibility of its fulfillment in history itself.

It is only by not avoiding implicit or explicit ideas of Monophysite or Nestorian nature that it is possible to evaluate the juridical-institutional dimension of the Church as a necessary phenomenon of the incarnation of the formal binding force of word and sacrament. This dimension *cannot* be reduced to a system of juridical norms always to be sidestepped in the name of another theological reality (principle of "economy"), nor to a purely sociological phenomenon, intrinsically unnecessary for salvation in faith and simply inevitable because of inescapable historical necessity ("mit eisernder Notwendigkeit," SOHM).

ORTHODOX THEOLOGY

There are various historical reasons to explain why Orthodoxy, aside from vague remarks emerging from the debate about the institute of *economy*, has never explicitly examined the problem of the theological foundations of canon law. First, it must be pointed out that the system of *symphonic* superimposition of Church and state, first elaborated by Justinian and lasting into the twentieth century, has never led the Orthodox Church to claim juridical autonomy for itself. The fundamental institutional autonomy of the Church was never denied by the Byzantine empire, nor by the Ottoman one, nor by any modern state, at least until World War II. The experience of the Western Church, while similar under the medieval feudal system, was different in its clash with illuminist Western states. We must also consider the fact that theological questions about the existence and the nature of canon law, raised by the Protestant Reformation and imposed by it on the attention of Catholic theology, have remained fundamentally extraneous to Orthodoxy. The Eastern Church has never surrendered to the temptation of separating the visible Church from the invisible one. In contrast to the Latin Church's propensity to pay great attention to earthly ecclesial realities, the Orthodox Church has always preferred to contemplate the ontology of the celestial realities.

In any case, there are many modern authors, both Eastern and Western, such as Evdokimov and Heiler, who have faced the question of the theological nature of canon law. Their discourse, however, is principally marked by the preoccupation with comparing the Eastern tradition to the Latin one. While these authors consider the Latin tradition to be affected by excessive legalism, their conclusions do not reach the same level of cultural and theological analysis as corresponding Catholic and Protestant attempts. In any event, these attempts to examine canon law can be interpreted correctly only if one succeeds in placing them within both the larger *nexus mysteriorum* proper to the Eastern theological system and the real juridical practice lived by the ancient and modern Orthodox Church. It would clearly be simplistic — especially if one intended to give an assessment of relative worth — to reduce the different ecclesial experiences, as some have done, and to present the Protestant Church as the Church of doctrine, the Catholic Church as the one of law and the Orthodox one as the Church of worship (SEEBERG). It is nevertheless impossible to deny the profound resistance of the Orthodox Church to any attempt at constricting the mystery of salvation within institutional and juridical schemes.

The Contemplation of Transcendence

Orthodox theology has always emphasized transcendence. After contact with third century neo-Platonism, but especially after the medieval Hellenistic-Byzantine reorganization that followed its encounter with the Slavic peoples, Eastern Christianity assumed a profound mystical value. This stood in marked contrast to the Western Church's assumption regarding the sacral but concrete mentality of the Germanic nations.

Although it is now possible to evaluate Orthodox spirituality — especially in today's church — without concentrating on monasticism alone, there is no doubt that it was in monasticism that the religious genius of the Christian East emerged in its most paradigmatic manner. Eastern monasticism differed from the Benedictine way because it was not guided by the desire to possess and dominate earthly reality through labor. Instead, it was driven by the desire to establish, above all, a relationship of the individual person with God (SEEBERG). Thus, Orthodox spirituality culminates in an aristocraticism inspired by the personal charisms of the monk who breaks with the social world because he hopes not for the world's transformation from within through his own labor, but only in the possibility of its transfiguration (CLÉMENT). In his *fuga mundi* [flight from the world], the Orthodox monk finds inspiration not only in the ascetic ideals typical of the primitive Church, but also in the cultural dualism of Eastern spirituality of Platonic inspiration (LOUVARIS). In the mysticism of the theosis or divination of the human being — the final goal of Christian purification — Orthodox spirituality has been able to transfigure also the contemplative experience of Eastern peoples.

Orthodox theology begins with a different anthropological perspective (BETH) and with a cultural infrastructure of Platonic derivation. It also maintains, however, a fundamental Pauline inspiration (CLÉMENT). Consequently, this theology does not follow the deductive type of conceptual knowledge valued by the West, but seeks sapiential knowledge which, instead of the desire to define, feels the need to avoid definitions (CONGAR). An icon does not assert an existence of its own because it does not claim to be an incarnation, but merely a sensible sign of invisible transcendence. The icon attests to God's presence in the world by representing the irrational archetypes of intelligible reality without pretending to materialize or reify them. The rigor of Orthodox canons safeguards the spiritual from any possible objectivization (EVDOKIMOV).

In the icon, it is not the ilemorphistic principle of the *universalia in rebus* that is expressed, but the Platonic *universalia ante res*. In the same way, Orthodox theology refuses to conceptually define the mysterious, but preserves mystery in all its postulative force. Thus, Eastern theology makes the passage of salvation from the divine to the human by paths quite different from those of Latin theology.

Orthodoxy rejects, first, the notion of *created grace* which, being replaced by a concept of the adoptive filiation of God, allows the idea of meritorious expiation to be introduced into the process of justification (EVDOKIMOV). Secondly, Orthodoxy refuses the Scholastic notion of *ex opere operato* which, in its turn, develops into that of *transubstantiation* — a concept that Eastern Christians accept only with much resistance (HEILER). These doctrines are based on the ilemorphistic principle of efficient causality; in them, there emerges the typical Latin attempt to rigorously and deductively apply the principle of the incarnation to all aspects of the economy of salvation. Orthodox theology prefers the idea of the deifying transmutation of *theosis*, where God communicates himself to humans not through his "essence," under the heading of the *analogia entis*, but through his "uncreated energies" (according to the doctrine of Gregory Palamas) in a superabundance of plentitude which, being personal, overcomes any need for created mediation (CLÉMENT).

Within this cultural framework, it was inevitable that Orthodox theology, in facing the problem of canon law, should not allow itself to be guided by the idea of fixing the incarnation of dogmatic truth in the juridical norm, an idea typical of Latin theology.

Universal and Local Church

The same Platonically derived reticence predictably emerges also on the ecclesiological level, both in the way Orthodox theology establishes the relationship between universal and local Church and in how it conceives authority within the Church itself.

Unlike Vatican II ecclesiology, which has not hesitated to define the local church as a *portio Ecclesiae universalis* (LG 23.2), Orthodoxy avoids considering the local church as part of the universal one (AFA-NASSIEFF). Instead, it stresses that all the particular churches are equal in manifesting the plentitude of the universal one. In the same way that there is a consubstantiality of all persons in salvation, there is also a Eucharistic consubstantiality of the local churches in the image of the most holy Trinity (CLÉMENT). If it is true that the local Church does not realize the universal one except by living in communion with all the others (*sobornost*) and that all these together form the universal Church, it is also true that the communion of the churches among themselves does not additively create a greater plentitude (EVDOKIMOV).

Despite the substantial convergence of these two ecclesiologies, one cannot fail to note the significant differences. Vatican II affirms with equal force the principles that the universal Church realizes itself in the particular one and, at the same time, is constituted by the particular ones, " ... *in quibis et ex quibis una et unica Ecclesia universalis existit*" [... in these and formed out of them that the one and unique Catholic Church exists] (LG 23.1). Orthodox ecclesiology Platonically tends to stress, more unilaterally, that the universal Church, ever the same and identical with itself, assumes the function of the archetype that realizes itself in the particular without ever being *constituted* as such by the plurality of particular churches (*"ex quibus"*). For Vatican II ecclesiology, it is essential that the universal Church, as archetype, should be ontologically constituted by the plurality of particular churches. This is a qualitative value and not an additive or quantitative one, and it is of a sociocultural or geographical nature. In fact, this is similar to the implicit principles underlying the conceptions of the *Oikumene* that the East has frequently advanced, and which the modern rationalist and illuminist West has translated into the category of pluralism.

From the Latin theological perspective, the hypothesis that a single particular church may freely realize the universal one could not be advanced, because the latter is not an abstract idea, but an ecclesial reality that is not only historically concrete, but which is also issues ontologically from the communion of all the particular churches. The Church of Jerusalem, for example, existed as the only Church, particular and universal at the same time; but this was true only on the historical plane and not on the theological one, as the entire plurality of particular churches was already embryonically present in the Apostolic "college."

This ecclesiological conception has precise implications for the nature of the communion existing among the particular churches. The *communio Ecclesiarum* is not only mystical but also structural and, therefore, juridical. Latin theology, with its marked sense for institutions, has defined this fact in terms of *communio hierarchica*. Indeed, all that which is structural is also juridically binding in and of itself. It follows that an ecumenical council cannot be considered, as Orthodoxy holds, merely as a place where mutual love is practiced (EVDOKIMOV); it is rather a place where the structure of the universal Church, necessarily resulting from the plurality

of particular churches, becomes binding in itself —
not because of any eventual acknowledgment or later
reception by autocephalous churches which, in this
way, would be the only ones to exercise a binding
authority on the juridical level. Catholicity is seen
by Orthodoxy as an exemplary and formal cause
which, dividing itself equally among all the particular churches, generates unity among them (EVDOKI-
MOV). The Latin Church, on the other hand, tends to
stress the dependence of authentic truth on the structural and juridical unity of the churches themselves.

In Russian ecclesiology, especially — perhaps
because Protestant structures of thought are echoed
in it — infallibility is unilaterally considered as
belonging to the Church; therefore, there is a lack
of an absolute criterion of truth (BULGAKOV). In this
view, the ecumenical council — or, in the same way,
the Bishop of Rome — cannot bind *ex sese*, but only
post factum (AFANASSIEFF). The decrees of a council,
although they are held by Eastern theology to be directly inspired by the Holy Spirit (KARMIRIS), bind
immediately only at the level of discipline. At the
substantial level, they remain in suspension until the
moment of their reception by the whole Church. Indeed, an ecumenical council does not exist because
it is constituted by the accredited representatives of
all the particular churches, but because it witnesses
to faith and reveals truth. It is not juridical unity,
determined first by the formal authority of the bish-
ops gathered in council, that guarantees the definition of dogma; rather, the guarantee is found only
in the truth itself, which is continuously made to
emerge by the presence of the Spirit.

This vision of the dynamic of conciliar decisions

undoubtedly points out the profound nature of the episcopal office, which consists in rendering witness to — rather than in voluntaristically deciding what is — truth. Nevertheless, this view overlooks the fact that the value of the witness offered within the *communio hierarchica*, which flows from the Apostolic succession, has a juridical binding force in itself, as the *locutio Dei attestans* itself. In acknowledging a relationship of hierarchical subordination among particular churches within the great autocephalous ecclesial realities while, at the same time, denying all jurisdictional primacy within the patriarchal pentarchy, Orthodoxy undoubtedly falls into a contradiction. While we should not unduly emphasize this contradiction, it must be acknowledged that the Orthodox image of the universal Church translates itself into the negation of an institutional authority, whether ecumenical council or bishop of Rome, within the Church that might define the truth of dogma in a stringent manner.

At the same time, it would be incorrect to affirm that Orthodox theology does not recognize that the Church, prolongation and continuation of the incarnation of Christ in history (KARMIRIS), has a real role in the mediation of salvation. Nevertheless, Orthodoxy firmly affirms that no human person may be considered head of the Church because Christ alone is the head (HEILER), thus betraying its reticence before the juridical-institutional phenomenon. Thus, it is symptomatic that Eastern theology never framed the distinction, which arose in the West especially with the School of the *ius publicum ecclesiasticum*, between the *postestas Ecclesiae propria* and the *postestas vicaria* that is exercised in Christ's name.

Because Orthodoxy begins by affirming that Christ alone is head of the Church, any juridical hypostatization — whether monocratic or collegial in type — becomes impossible not only at the level of the universal Church, but also at that of the particular one. Even at the the eparchial level, it is Christ who guides the Church through the bishop. This does not exhaust the whole plentitude of the Church, although the bishop is the *membrum praecipuum* without whom the Church could not exist, in the same way that human beings cannot exist without breath, or the world exist without the sun (*Confessio Dosithei*). Given that the universal Church, as archetypal reality, is not constituted by the existence of the particular churches, and given that it is not possible to hypostatize the authority of the Church in the person of the pope or, therefore, of the bishop, it is inevitable that the council cannot enjoy a juridical power *ex sese*, but only *post factum* — that is, after reception by the Church itself, whose sole head is Christ.

From these premises, it becomes clear that the ultimate problem for Orthodoxy resides in its being unable to accept the idea that dogma may translate itself in juridical terms in the same way that the icon, in its symbolic expressiveness, cannot be translated by rational categories. Latin theology, in turn, has established a total identity between theological and juridical truth in the dogma of the primacy of papal jurisdiction; in this theology, juridical formulation and theological truth are coessential (CONGAR).

The Principle of "Economy"

The principle of *economy* is perhaps the one that most clearly gives rise to the different conception of law held by the East. In its widest acception, the principle of ecclesiastical economy signifies the transposition of divine pedagogy and the methodology of salvation history onto the historical situation of the Church. God, who wishes to render human beings perfect in holiness by raising them to divine communion in *theosis*, realizes this plan in patience, mercy and forgiveness (MEILIA). This is the clear doctrinal premise, inspired especially by St. Basil, upon which both East and West have based the doctrine and practice of economy. It cannot be denied, however, that, in Orthodox theology, doctrine and practice have been and remain imprecise and fluid. Some modern theologians emphatically stress the specific Orthodox nature of economy. Nevertheless, on the basis of the definition of this institute that these theologians offer (e.g. KOTSONIS), it would be difficult to isolate substantial differences between it and those institutes of Latin canon law, (such as dispensation, *epikeia*, *aequitas*, privilege) that the more refined Western juridical expertise has used to sort and distinguish, from the Middle Ages on, the diverse juridical elements that make it possible to translate the idea of economy institutionally (CONGAR).

Undeniably, the Eastern and Western ways of understanding the phenomenon of law are profoundly different than the more widely accepted classical definitions of equity produced by Orthodox doctrine. Beginning with the strongly held view that there are no valid sacraments outside the one (Orthodox) Church (DUMONT), Orthodoxy's acknowledgments or denials of the validity of the sacraments of Baptism and Orders celebrated in heterodox churches was very uncertain and frequently contradictory. This phenomenon finds its roots not only in contingent political motivations but also undoubtedly in the fact that Eastern theology, in contrast to the Latin one, has never been able to distinguish precisely between order and jurisdiction. The failure to make such a distinction was probably due to the endurance of the system of relative ordinations. Indeed, the same uncertainty concerning the validity of the sacraments was also experienced in the West until the latter half of the twelfth century (STICKLER), until theology finally distinguished formally and terminologically the existence of two functions in the one *sacra potestas*. The first function, that of order, is conferred with the sacrament, and so can never be lost and, therefore, can always be exercised validly; the second function, that of jurisdiction, is conferred by the *missio canonica*, and in the system of absolute ordination can always be lost.

Explaining how the Orthodox Church has been able to accept or reject the validity of sacraments celebrated *extra muros* at different times, or those celebrated at the same time in different heterodox churches, is a preoccupation that clearly arises in the more extreme and divergent doctrines about economy. According to Thomson, ancient and modern Greek theologians hold that economy not only: 1) may render invalid that which is valid, but cannot render valid that which is invalid; or 2) cannot render invalid that which is valid, nor render valid that which is invalid; but may also, 3) render invalid that which is valid, but not render valid that which is invalid; or 4) render invalid that which is valid and valid that which is invalid.

Clearly, it is not possible to judge these antinomic solutions without taking into account the fact that Eastern theology has never been as determined as Latin theology to distinguish between an invalid and an illicit legal act or transaction. The Orthodox Church, moreover, despite the *acribeia* with which the letter of dogma is defended and the intransigent fidelity with which tradition is preserved, has always been distinguished by the tolerance and freedom it allows to theological opinions and by the elasticity with which it applies economy at the moral and canonical-disciplinary level.

Dogma and Law

This phenomenon of the balancing of opposites seems to be rooted in a deeper ecclesiological disarticulation. The Orthodox Church imposes on itself a great discretion in regard to the translation of the truths of dogma into conceptual terms. Faced by mystery, the Orthodox Church prefers to be engulfed by the silence of *apophania* (EVDOKIMOV). Sacrament, grace, and, consequently, canonical discipline, are considered as realities more immanent to the Church than revealed truth itself. Thus, Eastern theologians unanimously acknowledge that the Church may exercise a more extensive lordship and power of disposition over the sacraments and over grace than is granted by Latin theology, which gives to the

Church only a ministerial power (ALIVISATOS, CONGAR). This presupposition is undoubtedly one of the elements that explains the tendentially positivistic conception of canon law in Orthodoxy as it is presented by Evdokimov and confirmed by Heiler.

It is symptomatic that the Eastern theologians' discussion of canon law does not find its term of reference in the juridical system as such, but in the canons — that is, in the several positive norms. Their discussion does not make the distinction between *ius* and *lex*. This empiricism undoubtedly facilitates the fundamental affirmation, peremptory but ambiguous, that canons do not have a dogmatic character, nor can they be erected into a dogmatic system, because there is an otherness of planes and a constitutive diversity between dogma and law. The two are not to be confused (MARTINI and IPPOLITI). According to Evdokimov, the reason for this diversity resides in the fact that, between dogma and law, there is only a relationship of *functional reciprocity*. In this view, the canons are the external and visible expression of the dogmas, as if the juridical dimension existed only as an external dimension of the Church and did not belong, in the same way as dogma, to the metaphysical essence of the history of salvation. As a result, this external order is conceived in function of dogmatic teaching, with the task of organizing the charismatic element and of preserving it from any deviation that might touch upon the immutable essence of the Church. Clearly, this functional reciprocity is such that it risks emptying the institutional element of the Church of all intrinsic and direct soteriological value, degrading it to a purely formal element in the service of another reality, the charismatic one, as if charismatic reality were the sole substantial element of the Church's constitution.

These deductions are not consciously developed by Evdokimov. In rendering them explicit, however, we can clarify Eastern theology's approach to the problem of canon law. Canon law is considered a conditional or additional element that does not have a soteriological consistency of its own because it exists only in relation to another reality, which is therefore the only one that counts from the point of view of substance. Canon law, therefore, is ultimately seen merely as a socioecclesial superstructure — that is, a reality whose truth resides elsewhere, that is, in dogma.

A similar conception may perhaps be advanced for modern state law, in which the value of ethics, understood as a higher justice, is juxtaposed to positive law, which is considered to be a less perfect manifestation of true justice. In canon law, such a conception is not possible because neither dogma nor morality, insofar as they are capable of pointing out theological truth, are necessarily superior to canon law, as if they were its sole reason for, or source of, existence. Canon law is a reality in which the Church's experience and tradition become institutionalized; experience and tradition are not absolutely reducible to a purely doctrinal experience. Canon law, therefore, bears in itself at least a part of revealed truth, capturing a sense of truth with a logic and autonomy of means that are proper to canon law. In its relation to the ecclesial reality, canon law is not a sociological superstructure; it is an essential element through which the Church

becomes manifest in the binding force of total reality.
It has been justly observed that the otherness
between the two planes, the dogmatic and the juridical, is established by Evdokimov in accordance
with a Platonic model (MARTINI and IPPOLITI). Dogmas
represent the immutable of revelation; the canons
represent that which is moveable in the historical
forms. Eastern theology is as conscious as Catholic
and Protestant theologies of the historicity of dogmatic formulations (CLÉMENT). This being the case,
the use of the Platonic model clearly reveals the tendentially dualistic positivism with which the East
faces the juridical experience. The institute of ecclesiastical economy is the most characteristic manifestation of this dualistic positivism (DUMONT). In more
recent attempts, probably because of a preoccupation
with establishing convergent views, economy is
described according to a model similar to that of Latin
dispensation. If we leave these attempts aside, the
analogy between economy and the detachment or un-
concern for ecclesial realities will be clear; this is how
the Orthodox Church looks at secular earthly realities. Its affirmative response to the cosmos is, indeed,
only a relative one because, in the Pauline sense,
this is considered ephemeral and as the theater of
a purely provisional existence (LOUVARIS).

Especially at the turn of the century, grave accusations of quietism were leveled against the Orthodox Church by both Catholics and Protestants.
Without necessarily agreeing with these accusations,
one may legitimately note that, with regard to its
deepest tendencies and intentions, Orthodoxy certainly is not oriented toward the sociopolitical involve-
ment of the Church in the world, even as it affirms

that the world is to be seriously assumed to be the ethical instrument created by God for the realization of his kingdom (LOUVARIS). Even as generous a political proposal as Feodero's, which based its program on the slogan "the dogma of the Trinity is our political program," is unable to hide a certain Platonic innocence. The most authentically Orthodox temptation, which emerges most strikingly in monasticism, is undoubtedly that of abandoning the world to the logic of its own history (HEILER). Assuredly, this tendency has been one of the causes that has allowed the long coexistence of the Orthodox Church first with the empire and then with the state (SEEBERG).

Essentially, the Orthodox Church tends toward the contemplation of dogma as reflected in the symbolic splendor of the icon and as read through an "allegorized" ontology (DANIÉLOU), because transcendence is the only true reality (LOUVARIS). In the most authentic Orthodox conception, the Church is a mystical reality placed squarely in the beyond (SEEBERG) that transcends even its own institutional reality (LOUVARIS). Thus, if examined from the outside, the Church "may cause surprise through a certain relaxation of the forms and may give the idea of a certain neglect of earthly things" (EVDOKIMOV). It is not for nothing that only a conditional authority is granted to the law of order (ZANKOW). The canonical rule — rather than being seen as an instrument through which a correspondence between dogma and practice may be sought — is considered only as a model or "therapeutic ordinance" (Council of Constantinople II) that should be adapted to a personal and, therefore, unique destiny within an economy of mercy (CLEMÉNT).

The claim of the Latin Church that it wishes to establish, with absolute precision, a fully articulated correspondence between the awareness of dogma and the juridical order derives from the different Latin understanding of dogma itself. For the Latins, dogma is not so much a model to be contemplated in order to reach the transcendence of the triune God, a God whose "energies" can invest humans directly and divinize them in *theosis*, without the need of mediation through created grace. In the Latin view, dogma tends to be a categoric reality having in itself a formal binding force which, in accordance with the dynamic proper of ilemorphistic incarnation, necessarily finds definition in law. According to this view, the formal juridical value of canon law does not exhaust itself in the legal authority typical of secular law, which could not, in any case, monistically claim to be the sole model of juridical reality. The legal authority of canon law is like that of the *locutio Dei attestans*, which manifests itself through the particular modalities of sacrament and word — that is, of divine positive law. And canon law, without any break in metaphysical continuity, is the historical definition of divine positive law.

A paradigmatic example of the diversity between Eastern and Latin evaluations of the relationship between dogma and law is that of the indissolubility of marriage. The Latin Church has assumed the indissolubility of marriage as a given even on the juridical level, holding the binding force of its theological-moral value to be indivisible from the juridical-institutional one. The Orthodox Church, on the other hand, although proclaiming with absolute dogmatic persuasion the indissoluable *structure* of marriage, has never considered it necessary to translate this indissolubility onto the juridical plane. Orthodoxy applies the principle of economy, which is formally ruled by the criterion of equilibrium. This tends to guarantee the proportion between the celestial and earthly elements, between transcendence and immanence (LOUVARIS), and therefore induces caution about the sacramental nature of marriage after divorce (MEILIA).

The Orthodox Church, despite its dogmatic *acribeia*, possesses a liberalism that allows it to accept an almost limitless pluralism of theological opinions. The same transcendent/immanent dualism that is implicit in this liberalism emerges also in the practice of economy at the ethical and juridical-disciplinary level. It is true that the second marriage, by economy, is granted not through an administrative act, as is the case with Latin dispensation, but on the basis of a general law on marriage (L'HUILLIER), so as to avoid the danger of *empireia*. Nevertheless, it is evident that the law of divorce reveals in itself the dynamic appropriate to economy. This procedure, which is mediated through law, makes evident the extrinsic nature and, therefore, the ultimate positivism with which Orthodoxy faces the phenomenon of law.

The equilibrium between the celestial and the earthly tends to be independent of the resulting incarnation of the celestial in the earthly. Therefore, the earthly retains an autonomy of its own. This phenomenon, even when it is not the fruit of a hidden pessimism regarding the ethical value of earthly ecclesial realities, is the result of an ill-concealed rationalism that grants an autonomous human worth to these realities. Rationalism therefore becomes a dualistic dynamic. According to Orthodox theology, in order to save the *acribeia*, it is sufficient that, in the use of economy, the absolute value of dogma not be put in doubt; dogma must remain the archetype toward which all may address themselves. Nevertheless, this is ultimately impossible, except through a sort of Platonic abstraction. In the Latin Church, from the Protestant Reformation to the present, this same abstraction has led to the reemergence of the thesis, implicit in all the spiritualist movements of antiquity and of the Middle Ages, of the superiority of love and of charism over law and its formulations. The genius of the Western Church, which is more concerned with pedagogy and morality than with mysticism, has always sought to define the binding value of doctrinal truth by the operative concreteness of the juridical norm, incarnating the whole moral and operative potential charge of theological truth in the juridical system.

PROTESTANT THEOLOGY

Even with the intense theological efforts that have been made in recent decades, contemporary Protestantism continues to perceive canon law as a worldly and positivist phenomenon. This perception paradoxically issues from late medieval predestinational eschatology, in the tradition of Judaeo-Western Messianism. Protestant theology, while acknowledging that canon law is an unavoidable human praxis, is ultimately incapable of granting any salvific worth to it. This fundamental inability has its deep roots in the juxtaposition Luther established at a soteriological level between "Law and Gospel." On the plane of the history of salvation, this juxtaposition has found definition in the cosmic vision of the two kingdoms and, on the ecclesiological plane, it has resulted in the unbridgeable dualism between the "hidden" Church and the universal or visible one.

Protestant "hyper-eschatology" (EVDOKIMOV), which is immanent in the distinction between Law and Gospel, results, on the philosophical and cultural plane, in the legitimization of a historical praxis that lacks an eschatological dimension. Moreover, within the ecclesiological experience, this hypereschatology falls into the vision of a "hidden" Church that is so spiritualized that it transcends the history of the visible and sociological Church, without providing any means of establishing an intrinsic relationship between these two realities. In the Reformed theological system, the cosmic doctrine of the two kingdoms takes logical priority over that of the two Churches. This explains why Protestantism, until very recent times and in opposition to the Catholic tradition, has preferred to turn to the theology of law rather than to that of canon law.

Law and Gospel

It is well known that Luther saw the central point of the mystery of salvation in the theme of "Law and Gospel" (JOEST). In Pauline theology, the New Testament theme had resulted in the dialectical formulation of "Law and Christ." In reelaborating this theme, Catholic tradition had preferred the formula "Law and Grace" as more consonant with the fundamental tendencies of Latin theology.

The dominant preoccupation of Augustinian and Thomistic theology had been to establish both the unity between law and grace and the continuity of content between the Old and the New Law. The Old Law does not stand in opposition to the New because its essential contents endure even under the rule of grace. The New Law, on the other hand, differentiates itself from the Old because it is no longer *extrinsecus posita* — that is, imposed by intimidation on sinful humans — but is *intrinsecus data*, handed down along with the grace that gives us the strength to fulfill the law in the joy and freedom of love. St. Thomas, taking into account Pauline texts that are neglected by Luther, goes so far as to establish an identity between Law and Gospel, using the synthetic formula of the *nova lex evangelii: "Lex nova est ipsa gratia (seu ipsa praesentia) Spiritus sancti, quae (qui) datur Christi fidelbus"* [New law of the gospel: "The New law is the very grace (that is, the very presence) of the Holy Spirit which (who) is given to the Christian faithful] (*S.Th.* I–II, q.106 a.1). In any case, grace is law only in an analogical sense because the essence of the New Law does not reside formally on its legal character, but in the fact that it is given as grace. In defining Christ *as grace*, Catholic theology has wanted to underline the fact that the process of justification transforms a person internally. Grace is seen as an ontological reality communicated to individuals in order to give them the strength to fulfill the New Law, without abolishing the Old. Grace provides a progression from the natural to the supernatural law.

Moving within the nominalist and voluntarist horizons of the late Middle Ages, Luther defines Christ *as Gospel*. His view emphasizes the *non imputatio* of sin. Here, grace is a purely extrinsic, even if salvific, presence of Christ in the person. By substituting the formula of "Law and Grace" with that of "Law and Gospel," Luther, for whom the "supreme are of Christianity" consisted of being able to distinguish between law and grace, wanted to give expression to a twofold protest. First, he wished to condemn the Roman Church for having buried God's word and law under the law and word of the Church. Scholastic theology was his second object of protest, for it had replaced the idea of justification on the strength of God's justice alone with the idea of justification also by virtue of meritorious works done under the law and with the aid of created sanctifying grace. Luther would not admit that the economy of *sola gratia* might decay into a religious system still founded on law, where the works of natural law — even if done with the aid of grace — are required for justification. The works of natural law are not good in themselves; they become good when done in obedience to God who has saved us. Works, therefore, do not transform the person internally, but serve only to make manifest to others the miracle of God's forgiveness of sins.

In following Luther, Protestant theology has distinguished three uses of law. The first is the *usus politicus* in which, by God's will, law is imposed by the prince to impede the further corruption of humanity and a degeneration into chaos. The second is the *usus theologicus seu spiritualis* (or *elenchthicus*), by which law touches persons internally and more deeply than in the *usus politicus*, so convincing them of their own sinfulness. For Luther, this is the *usus praecipuus legis* because, considering that humans ever remain sinners, the law is essentially *accusans* (WOLF). The third use, the *tertius usus seu in renatis* (or *paraeneticus*), held by John Calvin to be the *usus praecipuus*, is that by which law, thanks to Christ's presence and aid, calls believers to a new life by giving them indications for salvation. Luther avoided treating this *tertius usus* because he held that justification on the strength of the Gospel is already, by itself, the root of a new life; where Christ is present, there is always birth and newness of life.

The notion of the *tertius usus* implies a view very near to the Catholic one of the *gratia elevans*, but the dispute that arose in the middle of the sixteenth century with regard to this issue drove Luther's followers to radicalize their position by separating the process of justification from that of santification. Philipp Melancton (1497–1560) tended to reduce justification to a simple amnesty by which God regards the sinners as if they were just; Nikolaus von Amsdorff (1483–1565) held that good works are harmful for the sanctification of the believer, while G. Major, on the contrary, affirmed them to be necessary. Faced by these contradictions, authors such as A. Poach and A. Otho antinomianly asserted that, since good works are spontaneously born of faith, law and its manifestations are superfluous. The *formula concordiae* of 1580 put an end to the controversy and provided the doctrinal bases for Protestant orthodoxy by turning again toward Luther's initial positions (LAU). Luther, however, by affirming that the good works done under the law are merely the fruit of the acceptance of the Gospel in faith, provided room for the doctrine that the works of the law are not necessary for salvation, not even as a *conditio a posteriori.*

From these positions, the theme of law progressively shifts toward moral theology and natural ethics. Melancton had already rediscovered the value of natural law and had partially reappropriated the Aristotelian tradition. The fact that all peoples had at all times known natural law was proof for him that human reason, although obfuscated after the original Fall, has not become totally corrupt. It follows that the relationship between the two kingdoms is not only extrinsic, as Luther had believed, but also intrinsic, and allows the establishment of a bridge between the law of God and that of nature.

The rationalist school of modern natural law theory, which, became important in the seventeenth century with Hugo Grotius (1583–1645) and Samuel Pufendorf (1632–1694), returned to this doctrinal tradition. This school transmitted many of the substantial elements of Scholastic theology; nevertheless, with Christian Thomasius (1655–1728), it developed features of Lutheran and Calvinist orthodoxy: the cultural isolationism, the acknowledgment of reason as the sole source of natural law, and the denial of the existence of all forms of divine law. Inevitably, therefore, the problem of the value of law was eliminated from the soteriological context of justification and from Christology, falling into the hands of philosophy and legal theory (IWAND). As a result, it is not surprising to find that the theological theme of Law and Gospel, which had made such a prominent appearance with the Reformation, found no space in such great theological works of the nineteenth century as those of Friedrich Schleiermacher (1768–1834), Albrecht Ritschl (1823–1889) and Adolf Harnack (1851–1930). This development was, of course, closely related to the radical shift in eschatology that took place at the same time in both Protestant theology and philosophical-social thought.

Luther's eschatology, dramatically present in his doctrine of *simul iustus et peccator* (PRENTER), was the direct consequence of the juxtaposition posited between Law and Gospel. Luther affirmed the thesis of human nature's irreparable corruption of the kingdom of the left hand and, consequently, of human or state law. He also asserted the radical otherness of the hidden Church in regard to the visible one and, therefore, the soteriological irrelevance of canon law. By these assertions, he encouraged a profoundly pessimistic conception not only of the world, but also of the visible Church; the latter was now deprived of the necessary intrinsic elements that could make it the locus for the verification of faith in history. This development furnished the premises for the progressive slide of the most advanced Protestantism toward a conception of history wholly devoid of eschatology.

Within Protestantism, eschatology became the inheritance either of the more orthodox currents or, especially in its millenarian and apocalyptic manifestations, of pietism and of the antiestablishment ecclesial movements throughout the world that separated from official national churches and broke into sects and free churches. The dominant Protestant theology, on the other hand, having been influenced by the Enlightenment and liberal rationalism, spiritualized eschatology so radically as to deprive it of all relevance, whether theologically or culturally, as happened with large sections of the pietistic movement. The so-called cultural Protestantism, with its inclinations toward Darwinist evolutionism and Christian socialism (PRENTER) — represented by the more illustrious thinkers of the nineteenth century, such as Weiss, Albrecht, Sohm and the others cited earlier — was then able to substitute history for eschatology and to identify the kingdom of God with the religious, cultural, political and social progress immanent in the destiny of the world.

The Doctrine of the Two Kingdoms

The Middle Ages, in continuity with the Gelasian doctrine of the "two powers," had developed a unitary system for explaining the ordering of the world. For the community of Christians, God has instituted a single spiritual temporal kingdom, the *Christian republic*; within this, there exist two separate, but reciprocally ordered, structures. The ecclesial hierarchy, culminating in the Roman pontiff, the supreme head of the universal Church, guides Christendom in the spiritual sphere; the temporal hierarchy, represented by the emperor of the Holy Roman Empire, guides it in the secular sphere. The unitary nature of this theological-political system is guaranteed by the superiority — spiritual, at least, if not necessarily jurisdictional (Gregory VII) — of the altar over the throne. There is, moreover, a correspondingly unitary conception of law.

In this system, the ultimate foundation of every

form of law is the *ius divinum*. In the intellectualist view of the system, the dominant role is assigned to the *ratio divina*, which gives origin to that *lex aeterna* from which the *ratio humana* derives the fundamental principles of natural law. In the voluntarist view, which stresses the biblical idea of divine immediacy in the production of law, the dominant role is assigned to the *voluntas Dei* as immediate source of natural law. In both these views, which find their balance in Thomistic realism, the dependence of the *lex humana* on natural law and the dependence of natural on divine law allows for the tracing of all human justice to a single source, divine law. The *ius humanum* is derived, through the mediation of natural law, from divine law and, therefore, is valid only if it is consonant with first principles (STIEGLER).

Luther, inspired by the Augustinian distinction between the *civitas Dei* and the earthly city and under the influence especially of the voluntarist nominalism of Gabriel Biel, chose to replace this order by another and turned the system over on its head. According to Luther, the order of salvation is constituted by two kingdoms. The spiritual kingdom, to which the believing Christian belongs, is governed by God's right hand, founded on faith and is guided by charity. The temporal kingdom, to which the nonbeliever belongs, is governed by God's left hand. It is ruled by reason *totaliter deleta* and is dominated by human power. Between the kingdom of the right hand, or *corpus Christi mysticum*, and the kingdom of the left hand, or *corpus babilonicum*, which was created by God in his *ira misericordiae* after the Fall in order to avoid humanity's degradation into total "chaos," there is an insurmountable abyss.

This dualism is ultimately overcome in the unity of the will of God, who has willed both kingdoms. Thus they do not exist purely as two heterogeneous realities. The relationship between them, however, is no longer intrinsic, but has become entirely extrinsic (voluntarism). God still rules the world with his word; this, however, is no longer the *verbum Dei ad nos* of the Middle Ages, but has become a *verbum Dei in nobis* (subjectivism). That portion of humanity that hears the word *spiritualiter* is granted God's justice in gift: these are the *iniusti iustificati*. The rest, who hear God's word only *carnaliter*, distance themselves from God and fall into damnation: these are the *iniusti non iustificati*.

To this dualism, there corresponds also a dualistic conception of law. In the kingdom of God, the *lex caritatis, seu spiritualis* or the *lex Christi* rules; this is addressed to the *homo interior* and can be perceived only with the *intellectus fidei*. This wholly spiritual *lex fidei* requires a purely interior conversion; external behavior is simply its spontaneous consequence (Christian freedom). In the kingdom of the unbelievers, the *regnum diaboli*, the *lex Christi* is no longer understood. Consequently, the law made by the state is no longer rooted in love but founded purely in power; it is addressed to the *homo exterior* and requires only external adhesion. This latter law is only a deceptive shadow of the divine one and, thus, is absolutely incapable of conquering human selfishness because, instead of granting forgiveness, it threatens vengeance and administers penalties — even the penalty of death.

In juxtaposition to the medieval tradition, then, Luther speaks of two natural laws: the spiritual and the secular. For St. Thomas, natural law had issued from principles that human reason could discover in the *lex divina*, the eternal plan preexisting in the *ratio Dei*. For Luther, there is no longer a *participatio legis aeternae* in human reason. Divine natural law is merely the juridical will of the God who commands and who will sit in judgment at the end of the world. The voluntarism of the late Middle Ages is conjoined in Luther with the eschatology of spiritualist movements. If human beings can no longer reach God by reason, but only in faith, God can reach them with his will and his law. This law, however, becomes binding only by a person's interior adhesion to it. The secular natural law that is produced by reason, even if it is willed by God, is wholly marked by human logic and by human justice: the justice of the Decalogue, the *lex Moysis*, is no longer a part of divine natural law for Luther, but is only an anthropomorphic and dim image of God's justice.

Modern interpretations of Luther's thought run along two opposing paths. Some believe they can affirm that, even for the Wittenberg reformer, secular natural law and the state are ultimately subject to Christ's lordship (HECKEL); others hold that the dualism between the kingdom of the right hand and that of the left hand is so radical as to exclude the possibility that the Gospel might furnish concrete indications for the juridical ordering of the state and of society (ALTHAUS). Whatever the correct position may be, the fact remains that in very recent times, the tendency of Lutheranism has been to rigorously separate Gospel and law, Church and state. This leaves to the state and to secular law a boundless autonomy with regard to the Gospel. This profound "disharmony" in Luther's teaching (WOLF) may have been at the root of the profound "demonization" of German politics from the nineteenth century onward.

The religious and cultural debate in the centuries following the Reformation has been characterized by divergent tendencies on the theoretical level. In several paradoxical ways, however, these tendencies have practically converged in a progressive abandonment of the world, giving it over to the logic of its own dynamic of secularization. On the one hand, there has been no dearth of movements which, within the Pietist movement, have theorized the necessity of withdrawal from all worldly and political engagement in order to cultivate a subjective interiority, reflecting eschatalogical expectations of a Messianic and millenarian nature. On the other hand, there has been the success of the political projects that were born of the encounter of Protestantism with the rationalism of the Enlightenment; in the modern state, territorial and absolutist, the state and its laws have been considered the exclusive sphere of a sovereign and immanent human reason. Until the end of the last century, these views found theological backing in the works of theologians such as Hernest Troeltsch (1865–1923) and Friedrich Naumann (1860–1919). Such writers continue to interpret the doctrine of the two kingdoms as a total separation between Christianity and politics. They can therefore make the assertion that, if the Beatitudes are to rule in the former, the latter is to be dominated by the power of law (SCHÜLLER).

Invisible Church and Visible Church

Analogous to the doctrine of the two kingdoms, Luther also formulated that of the two Churches, thereby establishing the profound separation between the Church *abscondita* or *spiritualis* and the universal one. Subsequent commentators have expressed this juxtaposition in terms of the visible and invisible Church.

Luther proceeded from the doctrine of the complete corruption of human nature and denaturalized that concept of *communio spiritualis* that was a part of late medieval penitential theology. This allowed him to develop the concept of *ecclesia abscondita, seu spiritualis.* Such a Church is the community of the just, whose members are known only to God, and it is wholly distinct from the external and sociological organization of Christianity, which is the universal Church, to which belong all the baptized, even if they are sinners. The first, the community of the just, is the vital principle; the second, the universal Church, is the field of action of the spiritual Church. In the first, only divine law is binding (*Ecclesia vivit iure divino*); it is a spiritual law that relates only to each person's interior sphere. The invisible Church cannot act as legislator because it does not have that power itself; it limits itself to the promulgation of Christ's judgment in penance and excommunication. This right is only meant for the invisible Church, and functions that are to be exercised by the external and juridical organization of the universal Church should not be associated with the invisible Church. For in the visible Church, only human or canon law holds sway, and it can bind humans only exteriorly. Because the law of the visible Church merely regulates the relationship between Church and individuals and of individuals among themselves, it exists on exactly the same level as the law of the state.

In theory, only the just are called to the creation of canon law, which retains its juridical character even if, unlike the law of the state, it cannot assume the binding character that is proper to law. If saints were the only members of the universal Church, canon law would be superfluous because it is not intrinsically necessary for salvation. Its justification is a purely moral one: it serves to assist the weak in the name of Christian charity. The binding force of the Church's precepts does not proceed from the formal character of either the law or of authority as such, but only from charity. Thomas Hobbes (1588–1679), in speaking of the law of the state, had been able to say: *"Auctoritas, non veritas, facit ius"* [Power, not truth, makes right]. For Luther, one would have to say: *"Caritas, non auctoritas, facit ius"* [Charity, not power, makes right] (HECKEL).

The fact that canon law is sanctioned and controlled by the believing faithful, who also have some part in the hidden Church, saves the principle of evangelical freedom and establishes an external connection with divine law. Nevertheless, there is no longer a guarantee of intrinsic unity between the two Churches. Canon law, is therefore, *sui generis*; it shares the trait of being an order of love with the divine law of the invisible Church, yet it is similar to state law because it refers only to the *homo exterior*. Finally, however, it differs from both of these other laws because, being a purely human law, it does not bind the believers in conscience. Although Luther acknowledged the concrete *need* for canon law, he irreparably severed it from divine law. The affirmation of belief in the Catholic Church (*credo ecclesiam catholicam*) applies only to the *ecclesia absondita*.

The juridical organization of the universal Church pertains to the duly constituted ecclesiastical organs. Nevertheless, in case of disorder — and only then — the prince as *membrum praecipuum ecclesiae* (Melanchton), may intervene in the process. Thus, already in 1525, Luther had asked the princes to take the juridical organization of the Church into their own hands and tutelage. In Germany, from that time until the end of the First World War, this juridicial power remained in the hands of the state so that canon law was substituted by ecclesiastical law (*Staatskirchenrecht*).

Not only the believers, but also those Christians who have lost their faith, live in the worldly kingdom, that of the left hand. In Luther's doctrine, therefore, the visible Church is *not* to be identified with the worldly kingdom. The visible or universal Church, rather, is a reality that stands between the kingdom of the right hand, this being identified with the invisible Church, and that of the left hand; it is a corpus *permixtum*. The invisible Church does not need any human law; the visible one, on the other hand, for empirical and sociological reasons, does need a canon law. In Luther's thought — and even more especially, in Calvin's — this law preserves an ecclesial dimension that differentiates it from secular law. Nevertheless, neither canon law nor the universal Church has any value in the order of salvation. Consequently, although the state does not enjoy any power over Christians merely by virtue of its own authority, believers are nevertheless to submit freely to the prince's power in the name of Christian charity. They must assume temporal offices, even if this entails facing the temptations of the *regnum diaboli*. According to the doctrine of the two kingdoms, the political commitment of the Christian is no longer a structural implication of faith, but only of charity (HECKEL). This helps to explain how Protestantism, in the name of an eschatology that saves at the end of time, could so easily surrender to the temptation of facing the world. Protestant moralism, according to Max Weber, has greatly stressed the value of professional ethics, but it has frequently given up the attempt to transform political and economic structures on the basis of faith.

During the four centuries since the Reformation, the teachings of the Reformers on canon law have undergone a profound transformation. Under the influence of the Pietistic conception of Thomasius, who denied the existence of any divine law, the following principle was formulated: the invisible Church is free of all law, whether divine or human; the visible one, on the other hand, because of empirical necessity, must accept a human law that ever more frequently finds its source in the state, given that the state had come to be considered the sole source of law (WOLF). Severed from the *ius divinum*, human law can no longer bind the Christian as such. In this way, the inevitable antinomy between law and charity, between the Church of law and the Church of love, between law and Gospel, is born.

The ultimately Platonic source of this antinomy

ought not to be ignored. *Epikeia*, a key concept for the comprehension of any doctrinal position on law (HARING), represented a positive correction of human law for Aristotle; Plato considered it a corruption in respect to the archetype of justice (HAMEL). Moving from the metaphysical to the more properly theological plane, Luther in turn considered all forms of human law, whether canonical or secular, as deceptive shadows of the divine law. For Luther, divine law transcends the human law but cannot possibly exercise an intrinsic influence on it, in the same way that the true and hidden Church transcends the visible Church without becoming incarnate in it.

The acceptance of the nominalist and voluntaristic theses of the late Middle Ages (Duns Scotus, Ockham, Biel) had driven Protestantism to abandon canon and secular law to a process not merely of profound scientific investigation, but also of purely rational and worldly positivization. Left in the hands of secular power, canon law becomes ecclesiastical law and undergoes a profound internal metamorphosis because of the rigorous application, especially in the nineteenth century, first of juridical-Pandectistic methods and then of the historical methods of secular juridical science. The inevitable hypertrophy suffered by ecclesiastical law, proportionally inverse to its intrinsic ecclesial value, brought about, on the institutional plane, the juridical absorption of the Church into the structure of the state and its transformation into a State-Church (*Staatskirche*). On the academic plane, the same process resulted in the elimination of every formal difference between canon and secular law.

At the end of the last century, Rudolph Sohm loudly

protested this state of things (ROUCO VARELA). Sohm's criticism was founded on two ideological presuppositions which, although quite different, were both profoundly rooted in the religion and voluntaristic spirit of Protestantism: first, the spiritualist view, according to which the Church is a purely charismatic society; second, the positivist view, according to which law is a monistic reality and there can be no diversity of nature between canon and secular law because the state is the sole source of juridical norms (Hegel). Beginning with a discussion of these views, Sohm rendered explicit the doctrinal implications of the disharmonic system of the two kingdoms and all its inexorable consequences. On the one hand, against Luther, he held that there is no difference between the visible or universal Church and the kingdom of the left hand, identifying the sociological Church with the world. On the other hand, he coherently denied not only that the Church may accept a divine law, which had already been eliminated by juridical science, but also a human law, since the latter could only be of secular derivation. With the central thesis of his *Kirchenrecht* I (1892), according to which "the nature of canon law is in contradiction with the nature of the Church," Sohm, for the first time in the history of theology, posed the theological problem of canon law. He did this in such radical and explicit terms that no respite was allowed for canonists, whether Protestant or Catholic, even to our own day (MÖRSDORF).

Gospel and Law

The definitive disintegration of the medieval order in Europe was brought about by the French

Revolution and its destruction of the sociopolitical structures of the *Ancien Regime*. This phenomenon caused the downfall of structures that had been considered vital not only by the Catholic church, but also by the Protestant church, and forced the churches to find a new historical starting point. Moreover, Romanticism led German Protestantism to rediscover not only its own origins, but also its own ecclesial conscience. This starkly revealed the distance that had come to exist between the constitutional and juridical structures imposed by the Illuminist state and the theological substance of the Church. The attempts at episcopal and synodal or presbyteral restoration of the last century were supported by several jurists, such as Stahl and Puchta and, eventually, also by the foremost exponents of the Berlin historical school, such as Richter, Friedberg, Hinschius and Kahl. Remaining bound academically by a monistic conception of law, however, these jurists went no further than to abstractly assert the autonomy of the Church in regard to the state, without considering the possibility of making this concrete by asserting the autonomy of canon law in respect to the law of the state (ROUCO VARELA).

Sohm's radical revolt defined the ultimate theological and juridical terms of the problem: what are the theological and methodological justifications of canon law? Is it possible that the need to clarify the problem was imposed, even more than by academic concerns, by the political developments in church and state relations that had taken place in the ensuing decades? The principle of the separation of church and state had been affirmed under the aegis of the Liberal revolution and by the programmatic

Constitution of Frankfurt (1848). Although that constitution was soon laid to rest by the triumph of the radical reaction and by the *kulturkampf*, the principle eventually found institutional embodiment in the Weimar Constitution (1918) and in that of Bonn (1949). Article 140 of the latter again asserted the abolition of the system of the State-Church and the right of "religious associations" to free self ordering and administration. These principles made it necessary for Protestant churches to promulgate their own constitutions, founded no longer on secular law, but on canon law. Responsibility for the juridical organization of the Church, handed to the state by the Reformers, four centuries later has returned to the competence of the Church.

The first theoretical attempts to again provide a theological legitimization of canon law followed the line of Luther's doctrine of the two kingdoms and the two Churches. Under Schleiermacher's cultural and terminological influence, Günther Holstein has drawn a distinction between the Church of the spirit, which is the body of Christ, and the Church of law, which is a sociohistorical manifestation and the locus for the juridical organization of the members of the Church. Although not contradictory, the two Churches are not identical because legislative power does not belong to the sociological Church, as if in a democracy, but to the Church of the spirit. Canon law, therefore, is a confessional and confessing law (*bekennendes Kirchenrecht*) that cannot make use of the institutes found in state, communal or parliamentary law, even if, in common with every other form of law, canon law has a purely human character.

Hans Liermann has also been unable to overcome

this "additive" solution (DOMBOIS), even though he has attempted to free himself from Luther's ecclesiological dualism. Although he abandons the terminological juxtaposition of Church of the spirit and Church of the law by affirming that the entire Church belongs to the content of faith, he merely substitutes a distinction between the Church as community and the Church as a society. Formally, canon law finds its validity not in its being "law," but only in its lack of contradiction to the nature of the Church. If canon law were to rely on state law, it would be unable to guarantee the fidelity of the Church to the Gospel or the Church's independence from the state. Canon law, nevertheless, remains a purely human and sociological law; its function is to serve the external discipline of the Church (WEHRHAN).

The disharmony in Luther's doctrine, according to which the visible Church is a *corpus permixtum* inadequately distinct from the kingdom of the left hand, has not allowed these authors to avoid all compromise with secular law. Having rejected Sohm's clear identification of the visible Church with the world, they have had to recognize that secular law, as the law of the kingdom of the left hand, is willed by God.

The incoherence inherent in Luther's dualism and the Nazi experience — which starkly revealed all the dangers inherent in the traditional institutional union between church and state in Protestantism — induced Karl Barth (1886–1968) to reject these early and failed attempts to justify canon law theologically. Barth proposed again that the central problem is the theological justification of secular law and not of canon law. In his famous lecture delivered at Utrecht in 1936, Barth sought to escape the blind alley in which Lutheran theology had found itself when pursuing the theme of "law and Gospel"; he inverted the terms of the question to "Gospel and law." Two years later, Barth again took up the theme in the program, "justification and law," and he proposed no longer a dualistic vision of the world, but a unitary one. Here, the Church and the state, with their respective juridical orders, are placed within the one existing reality, which is the salvific one of justification in Christ (SCHÜLLER).

Barth directly confronts historicism and legal positivism, which had suffered an extreme loss of prestige with the rise of Nazism. Barth's background is that of dialectical theology, in which the central problem is that of establishing the nature of the God/human relationship and whose starting point is not in the *theologia naturalis*, but in the realization that God is God in that he faces human persons with their own limits. Rational ontology and natural law are not useful in the understanding of God's otherness; revelation alone can formulate binding affirmations. Paralleling the biblical concepts of creation, original sin and reconciliation, the category of *justification* is the one that best expresses the nature of the relationship, not only of God with the Christian, but also of God with the human person. Justification takes place through Christ who, aside from being the ontological foundation, is also the *gnosis* of all created reality.

In greater agreement with the Calvinist than with the Lutheran tradition, Barth abandons the doctrine of the two kingdoms and the two Churches and supplants this with the vision of a single kingdom of God. Christ stands at the center of this kingdom, and all of reality is placed around this center in concentric circles. The Church stands closer to the center; the state stands farther away. Thus, there is no longer an absolute difference between church and state, nor can their relationship be seen, in accordance with the Catholic tradition, as if the Church were founded on divine law and the state on the natural one. Barth substitutes the *analogia entis* with the *analogia fidei*. This means that all of reality — not only the Church, but also the state and law as the regulation of human intersubjective relations — may also be understood in the context of the relationship of justification established by God with humankind. This single reality can only be known through faith and not by philosophy. No human metaphysics — whether Platonic, Aristotelian or Hegelian — is capable of defining the nature of the state.

Ernst Wolf came to share Barth's radical pessimism concerning natural law and went further by adding that the theology of the state and of law cannot even rest on the Stoic metaphysic found in Calvinism, as the witness of Scripture cannot be used to confirm the results of rational investigation. Moreover, he asserts that theology must be, above all, critical of philosophy (SCHÜLLER).

Reappropriating again Calvin's ecclesiology, Barth shifts the focus of attention from the universal Church to the local one. The community of Christians (*Christengemeinde*), by being closer to Christ, is capable of better understanding the meaning and nature of the political community (*Bürgergemeinde*), that is, of the state and its juridical ordering. Because the state has the function of guaranteeing an external juridical order that makes possible the preaching of the Gospel, the Church cannot remain neutral in its regard and, in a subsidiary way, is invested with a political responsibility (*politischer Gottesdienst*).

In consonance with the whole Protestant tradition, Barth rigorously reaffirms that, in the Church, the primary operating subject is not the community of Christians as such, but Christ himself. The community, therefore, has not a law unto itself, and canon law must be formed in the obedience of the Christian community to Christ. Nevertheless, it remains a purely human law because the obedience of the Church remains, at best, equivocal, imperfect and provisional. Its law is distinct from that of the state because it does not have the formal binding force that is proper to law; it remains purely an order (*Kirchenordnung*) that is ever reformable (*ecclesia semper reformanda*). Since the law of the state is born at an even greater distance from Christ, it is even less coherent and prophetic than canon law. Ecclesiastical law produced by the state is, therefore, radically incapable of providing the Church with an adequate juridical organization.

In any case, canon law, like every other form of law, is irreparably human because it is valid only for the time that separates the Church from the end of the world. Without facing directly the problem of whether canon law, in the formal aspect, is a phenomenon substantially different from state law, Barth affirms that it is a *sui generis* law because it is essentially a liturgical law, subject to the indications of Scripture and valid only as a "service" to the *communio sanctorum* and as prophecy in respect to the law of the state.

The Barthian theme of "Gospel and law" has been taken up not only by Ernst Wolf, but also by Jacques Ellul, who has introduced a clear distinction between natural law and the philosophy of law. Pointing out the chronic failure of the philosophy of law in more than 2,000 years of history, Ellul affirms that natural reason, *totaliter deleta*, is incapable of making valid and definitive assertions about natural law. Most importantly, this law, like religion and the state, exists as a human phenomenon and precedes any attempt at theoretical reflection about it. Thus, any judgment regarding the worth that human justice and natural law may have before God pertains to theology and not to philosophy. This examination of natural law by reference to Christ's revelation allows for the formulation of a theological foundation for any form of law, whether of the state or canonical. In any case, in the face of God's justice, human justice will always remain a non-law. It is only within the context of justification, where the human being is *simul iustus et peccator*, that human law, by an act of grace, is clothed with the justice of God.

Barth and Wolf had denied all substance to natural law; on the other hand, they had granted an important role to natural conceptuality and the immanent rationality of theological thought (SCHÜLLER). To avoid this contradiction, Ellul seeks to do without all intellectualistic presuppositions and formulates an option that is strongly nominalistic and voluntaristic. In particular, he attempts to eliminate those presuppositions that had emerged in the Scholastic tradition with Gabriel Vásquez and in modern natural law tradition with Grotius. These presuppositions had allowed for the affirmation that, *"etsi non daretur Deus, esset tamen iustitia"* (SCHÜLLER). Ellul affirms, instead, that human justice exists only as an expression of the judgment of God, because only that which is consonant with the will of God is just. Nevertheless, human justice is not static; it is dynamic because it manifests itself in God's present and concrete judgment, and it is a pure act of grace (dynamic voluntarism).

In conclusion, it must be noted that Barth, by turning Luther's position around, affirms that law does not stand in contradiction to the Gospel. There is unity between them because law is also revealed by God in Christ. Both are expressions of the grace that is God's word. Thus, there is opposition only if there is an "ill-understood" law. In itself, law is no more than the necessary form of the Gospel whose content is grace. In stressing the unity between Gospel and law and in again including canon law in the contents of faith, Barth makes a great leap forward toward St. Augustine and St. Thomas's conception of the *nova lex evangelii*. Nevertheless, Barth is not able to reestablish the unity between divine and human law. Even as he turns around the theme of Law and Gospel and abandons Luther's cosmological and ecclesiological dualism, Barth, in the final analysis, accentuates the Protestant dualism between the natural and the supernatural and between reason and faith. The separation between human law and the the divine one is a purely institutional consequence of this dualism.

Christology and Trinitarian Doctrine: The New "Loci Theologici" of Canon Law?

The Barthian exploration of "justification and law," by its inexhorable condemnation of natural law, had resulted in an impasse. Some jurists of the postwar period, having accepted that a theology of state and canon law could not be developed on the sole basis of revelation or without granting a role to metaphysics, have sought new methodological approaches, without explicitly addressing the other fundamental questions traditional in Protestant theology. Despite substantial systematic and conceptual differences, these authors, in disagreement with Sohm, directly confront the problem of the theology of canon law without first facing the question of the theology of law in general. Methodologically, they also place the problem of canon law before, or at least on the same level with, the ecclesiological problem (STEINMÜLLER).

Symptomatic of the discomfort caused by Barth is the fact that Johannes Heckel has again proposed, as *locus theologicus* of canon law, the Lutheran doctrine of the two kingdoms, and he presents this as a faithful interpretation of Luther. Nevertheless, Heckel is not able to provide a theological principle to show that divine law, or *lex charitatis*, heteronomous with respect to human law, necessarily postulates the existence of the canon law of the particular church, this being in turn a purely human law (ROUCO VARELA).

Heckel attempts, in line with Günther Holstein and Hans Liermann, to provide more than a purely sociological justification in order to root canon law more deeply in the structure of the economy of salvation. His has not been the only such attempt. Erick Wolf has proposed Christology as the new *locus theologicus* for a theology of canon law. His Christocracy is distinguished from Barth's because it receives the findings of a new-Kantian and phenomenological-existentialist philosophy as local presuppositions. In Wolf's view, divine law is essentially structured as "brotherly lordship" of Christ over humankind (*bruderschaftliche Herrschaft*). Divine law, finding definition in the Bible as Christian brotherhood, determines the nature both of canon law, which is therefore a law of neighbor (*Recht des Nächsten*), and of the Church, which is the historical locus in which the Christian's paradoxical experience is realized. Within these formal limits, canon law, in its material contents, continues to be a purely human law.

Hans Dombois takes the same approach. He believes the failure of Protestant and Catholic theology to resolve the problem of the law of the Church can be attributed to the exclusive use of abstract juridical categories (STEINMÜLLER). He substitutes anthropological-phenomenological concepts such as existence, person, structure, history and relationship. The human person, determined by the model of trinitarian relations, is constituted by four fundamental relationships: with God, man, woman and things; at the institutional level, these become Church, state, marriage and property. The institution is born of a dynamic founded on *traditio* and *acceptation* which, on the ecclesiological plane, become *ordinatio* and *iurisdictio*. The institutionalization of the God/human relationship in the Church is then the model for all other relationships. The juridical dimensions of this paradigmatic relationship emerge from the biblical categories in which God has expressed himself, and which are mostly juridical in origin — such as justification, grace, testament, witness and apostolate. The fact that God, in his relationship with humankind, should descend into history is an act of grace. Canon law, whose *locus theologicus* is the Trinity, is, then, a law of grace (*Recht der Gnade*). The ecclesiological weak point of this system lies in the fact that Dombois, adhering to the subjectivistic Protestant tradition, ultimately makes the existence of the Church as an institution dependent on its *acceptatio* by humankind. Hence, it follows that canon law has a purely human character and, once again, can be justified only on the basis of anthropology (ROUCO VARELA).

Critical Observations

The central point of convergence between modern Protestant theology of canon law and Catholic theology is the affirmation that canon law is a dimension of the Church that is indissolubly bound to dogma. As an ecclesial reality, therefore, not only does canon law belong to the content of faith — from which Luther had ejected it — but it is also at the very core of the issues that have garnered most of the attention of modern theology. Nevertheless, to pass silently over the deep divergences that still exist would be a facile surrender to the temptation of ecumenical ironicism.

The problem of canon law was raised by Luther's doctrine of the two kingdoms and the two Churches and by the opposition he established between Law and Gospel. These views resulted in Sohm's radical denial, as well as the inversion of the terms that Barth proposed, which was not a satisfactory solution to the problem. Barth *was* successful in again placing secular and canon law within the content of faith, inserting them as elements proposed and judged by revelation in Christ, which is justification. Nevertheless, because of his opposition to natural law and philosophy, Barth was unable to reestablish that unity among divine, natural and human law that had been asserted by the Middle Ages. The thesis of the unicity of the kingdom of God centered around Christ was not sufficient to eliminate the dualism between divine and human law. In the Barthian view, divine law is wholly transcendent, while human law remains a purely human reality. Thus, the dualism simply moves from ecclesiology to law.

The more recent attempts of Erick Wolf and Hans Dombois to resolve this problem have not been successful, either. In both writers, a platonic element emerges, as divine law — whether structured as Christ's "fraternal lordship" or as a "trinitary relationship" — is seen solely as a model according to which human law must structure itself, with the external assistance of biblical indicators (*biblische Weisung*). In Protestant theology, and especially with Calvin, these biblical indicators (*Weisung*) have substituted the principle of the incarnation for human law.

Essentially, Protestant theology, from Luther to modern theologians, has understood divine law in such a spiritualized sense that it is impossible to see how it might be binding for the historical Church. Protestant theology is unable to establish a binding relationship between the Christian and the Church;

it formulates instead a direct relationship between God and the human conscience. Canon law remains an inexhorably human law, incapable of binding the conscience of the Christian. A significant reason for this is the fact that canon law, not being granted a natural existence as an anthropological reality, also cannot be granted a soteriological existence. The antinomy between Law and Gospel deprives the law of all soteriological value. This devaluation cannot be overcome by a simple inversion of the terms, as Barth thought, or by making the value of the law dependent on the Gospel. The problem of the value of canon law cannot be resolved unless one first resolves that of the relation between reason and faith, the natural and the supernatural, history and eschatology. Even in some streams of Protestantism that were wary of the liberal rationalism of the eighteenth and nineteenth centuries and of eliminating this rationalism from eschatological history, a vision of eschatology persists that is wholly projected toward the future. In respect to the phenomenon of law, such a vision gives rise to a positivism analogous to that of Orthodoxy, in which eschatology can become simply an escape toward transcendence. Such traditions tend to abandon history to its own worldly logic.

At a basic level, Protestantism asks whether or not a theology can be developed without regard to any ontological-philosophical background. In particular, insofar as law is concerned, the problem is whether a theology of law must be primarily a theology of canon law, or whether it is necessary to make the theology of canon law dependent on a theology of law.

CATHOLIC THEOLOGY

Law and Grace

The response of Catholic theology to the problem of canon law is also to be included within the wider discussion of justification, a discussion that is crystallized in Luther around the juxtaposition of Law and Gospel and, in the Catholic tradition, in that of Law and Grace.

What does "Law and Gospel" mean for Catholic theology? Gottlieb Söhngen is one of the very few Catholic authors who has faced the question analytically and in dialectical relationship with Protestantism. According to this German theologian, the first necessary acknowledgment is that, in Catholic theology, as in Protestant, the conjunction *and* does not mean *also* because the intrinsic nature of the two realities is not identical. The essence of the law resides in its imperative character, while that of the Gospel and of grace resides in a participation of God in the heart of the human person. Thus, there is no *analogia nominum* by which it may be said that the law is also Gospel and the Gospel is also law, but only an *analogia relationis* (BARTH) established by the fact that the imperative of the new law — which is not law simply because it is formally law — finds its foundation in grace and charity. This relationship was expressed by St. Thomas, who used the formula "*nova lex evangelii*," thereby offering a synthesis of the preceding tradition expressed in St. Augustine's, "*da quod iubes et iube quod vis.*"

Thus, the novelty of the new law does not reside in its being more perfect than the ancient one, but in the fact that it is given as fullness of charity: *"Lex nova est ipsa gratia (seu ipsa praesentia) Spiritus sancti, quae (qui) datur Christi fidelibus"* [The New Law is the very grace (that is, the very presence) of the Holy Spirit which (who) is given to the Christian faithful] (S: Th. I–II, q. 106, a. 1). There is no *analogia nominum*, therefore, even between the Old and the New Law because, if it is true that Christ is not only mediator but also legislator, as the Council of Trent affirmed (Sess. IV *de iustif.*, can. 31), he is certainly not the type of legislator that Moses was. It is impossible, therefore, to justify the existence of canon law in the same way as the Old Law, as Luther attempted to do, merely as a bulwark against concupiscence and sin. Canon law belongs to the Christian experience in a positive way, under the sign of the fullness of charity and grace. It belongs to the tradition in the same manner as dogma, which, as we have seen, is not a heterogeneous reality in respect to law; just as salvation does not come from the formal imperative force of the Church's juridical order, law does not come from the pedagogical force of dogma, but exclusively from grace.

Grace, then, comprehends law and not vice versa, because the fulfillment of the law is not the efficient cause of grace. Medieval canonists had already precisely understood that grace transcends law when they dared to identify the *aequitas canonica* with God himself: *"Nihil aliud est aequitas canonica quam Deus"* [Canonical equity is nothing else than God] (Bolognese Gloss). Thus, the nature of *aequitas canonica* is profoundly different from the "Roman," as it makes reference not only to the norms contained in positive law, but also to other principles, such as

God himself and the Gospel (FEDELE).

If it is true that the Gospel is not *also* law, it is also true that the Gospel does not exist *without* law. As was true of the Old Testament, the New Law also is not given without the promise of grace, and grace is not given without the precepts of God. In the New Testament, grace cannot endure without the works of charity. Not even for Luther does the *sola fide* principle mean that faith can exist *without* works. The difference between the doctrine of the Reformers and that of the Catholics, as fixed by the Council of Trent (cc. 29, 30), resides in the fact that, for Catholics, works are not only a necessary *consequence* of faith, but a real and proper *condition* for salvation. In the two theological positions there are, therefore, points of convergence: salvation is granted by grace, and works are necessary. For the Reformers, good works — which are not good because they save, but only because they are done in obedience to God — are necessary only as a consequence. Moreover, good works are not to the advantage of those who do them, but to others who can see the miracle worked by God in salvation. For Catholics, on the other hands, works are necessary, at least as an *a posteriori* condition, even if they can be achieved by the believer only through the force of grace and faith, so that salvation should not turn into damnation. This does not mean that God forgives the sin of humans after they have forgiven others; rather, it is only the strength of the fact that God has forgiven them that believers are able to, and must, forgive others (SÖHNGEN).

This difference in the conception of the *conditio* derives from different ways of understanding grace. Especially in modern Protestant teaching, grace is not a simple *non imputatio* of sin, but an external personal presence of Christ. Therefore, while grace leaves believers unchanged internally (*simul iustus et peccator*), it involves them and renders them capable of loving, in the sense that Christ himself works in them (PANNENBERG). For Catholic theology, conversely, grace is a created supernatural reality infused in human beings as an inherent quality (*gratis creata habitualis*) which, diverging from Orthodox doctrine, is not to be identified with God (*energies*). Grace is a force that leads believers to act in cooperation with God (*fides charitate formata*), so meriting also an increase of such cooperation. The Protestant notion of *non imputatio*, while not denying the real efficacy of grace, rejects its being in some way causal and an ontological reality inherent in the human person. Rather, people are involved as instruments of God's action and not as collaborators. Moreover, the same view may be discerned on the ecclesial plane, where the Church does not have its own subjectivity because the sole operating subjects are Christ and the Holy Spirit.

Having posited the premise that grace does not become ontologically "incarnate" in human nature as *gratia creata* and that the hidden Church has no necessary correspondence with the universal or visible one, Protestant theology cannot establish a connection between divine and human law. As good works are only an external consequence of grace, so canon law is only an external consequence of the hidden Church. If canon law is necessary, it is so only on the sociological plane and not on the ontological one. Like good works, canon law has no specific value in itself. Like the Sacraments, canon law is merely a *signum fidei*, not an efficacious instrumental cause of grace. Clearly, the parallel between law and sacrament excludes the application of the principle of *ex opere operato* to law.

In hylemorphic Aristotelian and Thomistic metaphysics, the Catholic tradition has found an ontological and logical framework for rationally justifying its own form of belief in the mystery of salvation. Consequently, if only by analogy and differentiation, this tradition has applied the principle of incarnation — which finds its paradigmatic plenitude only in Christ — to all levels of the economy of salvation. Thus, this principle is applied rigorously not only to created grace, the Church and the Sacraments, but also to canon law. Divine law is present in canon law not purely as formal background from which the admonitory indication proceeds, but also as an ontological substratum. It is true that, as St. Thomas says of the Sacraments, all institutional realities in which grace becomes "incarnate" — such as the Church, the Sacraments, dogma and law — are merely *signa fidei*. Nevertheless, this is true because these realities are structurally efficacious signs of God's own grace. Because the application of the principle of incarnation leads to such conclusions, the Catholic tradition has clearly been able to view eschatology as a reality that is not only present in history, but which also constitutes the ultimate truth of history.

Methodological Developments

The ecclesiological and juridical dualism of the Protestant Reformation has its roots in Luther's juxtaposition of nature and grace, reason and faith, history and eschatology, "law and Gospel." The Catholic tradition, on the other hand, even amidst a variety of interpretations, has always preserved the unity of these elements. This unity is not simply extrinsic, by way of the unity of God's will, but also intrinsic.

The fact that law has always been considered an indispensable condition for salvation explains how the Catholic Church, "from a constitutional point of view, has never lived on precarious juridical bases" (ROUCO VARELA). It is not surprising, therefore, that the Catholic Church, whether in medieval Christendom or in times of state absolutism, has always asserted its own constitutional structure and juridical order, rooted in divine law and, therefore, autonomous. When the liberal nineteenth century state imposed separation, the problem for the Catholic Church was not that of finding a new constitutional framework to support its religious existence sociologically, as was the case for the Protestant Church. Instead, the Catholic problem was that of defending, as in previous times, the preexistence and the theological and institutional autonomy of its juridical order.

Even the antinomian crisis that has hit the modern Church, in the final analysis, has not placed the existence of institutions and of law in doubt, but has required a historical reformulation and a renewed grounding of these elements in theology. Proof of this lies in the enormous production of legislation that has taken place in the particular churches over the last few years. Through the participation of modern synodal and pastoral institutions, these legislative conclusions have been sustained — even by the more critical grassroots members of the ecclesial community.

The problem for Catholic theology, then, is not to theologically prove the existence of canon law because, in the final analysis, this is not even an academic question. Rather, the task is to provide a theologically correct justification of a reality that already belongs to the content of faith, if not always at the level of practice, at least at that of theoretical consciousness. The problem, therefore, is one of method. Canon law must be justified not on the basis of natural law or of social presuppositions, but from a purely theological starting point. The precise isolation within the *nexus mysteriorum* of the *locus theologicus* of ecclesial law would serve to eliminate from public discussion the existence, affirmed in practice in popular treatments of the subject, of an antinomy between law and freedom, institution and charism, law and grace.

It must be acknowledged that modern theological and canon law studies, with rare exceptions, have found themselves defenseless when trying to formulate a necessary and plausible response to criticism within the Church. Canonists have especially felt the lack of a unitary theological notion of law. Such a notion could become an interpretive category to use in synthetizing all the elements involved in theology's traditional approach to the concepts of law and justice. This unitary concept of law could also establish the exact relationship between the Church and law, with law as the element that determines the Church's sacramental being and existence as the *signum elevatum in nationibus*.

Rouco Varela has observed very astutely that there

are many more or less heterogeneous variants of the idea of law in the different branches of biblical, historical, or systematic theology. Thus, in soteriology, we treat God's justice; in sacramental theology and in ecclesiology, *ordo* and apostolic succession are touched upon; in moral theology, there are discussions dedicated to *de lege* and to *de iustitia et iure*. Moreover, in areas such as political theology, there are even attempts to implicitly grant a central hermeneutical function to the category of law in the treatment of theology as a whole. The science of canon law itself, however, provides no theological definition of its own *obiectum formale quod*. It is satisfied with founding itself on the notion of law underlying the 1917 *Codex Iuris Canonici* (CIC), which was formulated by Suárez as a synthesis of preceding Christian philosophical thought.

Medieval and modern canonical science define law as the category of the *iustum*, or of the *objectum virtutis justitiae*. It is evident that this definition, being philosophical in origin, is not able to explain the internal juridical structure of the Church. Canonists have sought to establish the connection with its soteriological dimension by determining the *sub gravi* or *sub levi* obligations imposed on the Christian conscience by canon law (ROUCO VARELA). The most evident expression of this approach is found in Suárez; he not only established, with Bartolomeo Medina and Thomas de Vio Cajetan, that the state may bind the fulfillment of external actions in conscience, but also that the ecclesiastical legislator may impose the performance of purely internal acts as an obligation. An example of the latter contained in the 1917 CIC (can. 593) is the injunction to the religious to strive toward perfection. Such an approach in defining the formal notion of the law is clearly insufficient for establishing a connection between theology and philosophy; at most, it does so with regard to philosophy and moral theology. The resulting ambiguity has created a profitless confusion between the methodological and epistemological basis of canon law and that of moral theology.

In the eighteenth and nineteenth centuries, the natural law theorists of the *ius publicum* furnished the instrument used by the illuminist and liberal state to impose its own exclusive territorial and juridical sovereignty on all sectors of social and ecclesiastical life. Catholic forces responded to this substantial and methodological challenge by creating the new science of the *ius publicum ecclesiasticum* (DE LA HERA). Its novelty resided in the elaboration of a juridical discipline that used a different methodology than classical canon law. For the first time, in the study of the *ius publicum internum*, the problem of the nature of the law of the Church was faced, finally bypassing the medieval *status quaestionis.*

The central category of the treatises of the *ius publicum ecclesiasticum*, concerning the *societas perfecta*, did not mediate a theological understanding of ecclesial law. This failure was due to its grounding in natural law theory and to its acceptance of the axiomatic assertion *"ubi societas ibi et ius"* as the major premise of the syllogism that proves the existence of ecclesial law. Aside from also being of natural law origins, this premise uses the same formal concept of law as the preceding canon law tradition. This methodological ambiguity arose from the desire to find scriptural confirmation for the basic principles of the philosophy of the state so as to be able to apply them to the Church. This attempt used a preconceived and secular view of law, extraneous to the so-called *hierarchological* passages of the New Testament. Moreover, this ambiguity has a clear connection with the theological nature of those times, when the principal preoccupation was the demonstration of the correspondence of reason with revelation.

The fact that the nineteenth century inverted the problem in order to demonstrate the correspondence of revelation with reason explains the progress achieved by the *ius publicum ecclesiasticum* with the Roman School of Camillo Tarquini (1810–1874) and Felice Cavagnis (1841–1906). They eliminated the more glaring elements of the Würzburg School natural law theory from their works, seeking a better — if still clearly artificial — scriptural and theological foundation for their treatises. In the final analysis, however, the connection between the Church as perfect society and ecclesial law rests not on the internal structure of the Church as such but, voluntaristically and extrinsically, on the will of Christ. Christ would have wished to constitute the Church both as perfect society and as juridical society.

Despite an attempt to overcome them, the same methodological limitations are discernible in the canon law studies of Georg Phillips (1804–1872). In line with German Romanticism and the political restoration of the first half of the nineteenth century, Phillips defined the Church by substituting the category of *societas perfecta* with the biblical one of *regnum*: the Church is Christ's kingdom on earth. Starting with a political and institutional preconception of "kingdom," this German canonist deduced the existence of a juridical order in the Church, founded on the unity of ecclesiastical power.

The limitations of the modern and lay Italian canon law school, from the theological perspective, are much more serious. Sharing the juridical and apologetic aims of the *ius publicum ecclesiasticum*, this school has attempted to demonstrate the juridical validity of the canonical order with respect to that of the state. Despite being one of the most brilliant efforts ever made by canon lawyers, this attempt represents a regression. Basing itself on the underlying category of the *societas perfecta*, it has sought to found canon law on the canonical system itself, but without the theoretical acceptance of something like Kelsen's "pure theory of law" (*Reine Rechtslehre*). The concept of "primary juridical order" underlies the School's whole scientific foundation.

Although this concept does not seem to derive from any philosophical presuppositions, it is borrowed — after the rejection of the more objectionable features — from the German Pandectistics of the last century which, having come out of juridical positivism, developed the science of the "general theory of law" (*allgemeine Rechtslehre*). However, when Italian canonists have been faced with the need to account for the specific nature of canon law with respect to state law, they have had to acknowledge the "epistemological incapacity of their methodology (ROUCO VARELA). Thus, declaring that the problem of the theological foundation of canon law is a parajuridical problem, they have left its solution to theology (DE LA HERA).

The problem has emerged most clearly in the discussion of the theme of *salus animarum*, which is considered by the Italian School as the final end of the canonical system (FEDELE). Members of the Italian School (D'AVACK) and of the Roman Curia School (BIDAGOR, BERTRAMS, ROBLEDA), wishing to overcome the excessively eschatalogical and individualistic (and, therefore, juridically extrinsic) elements of the *salus animarum*, attempted to provide a correction by substituting this concept with that of *bonum commune ecclesiae*. The problem, however, remains unsolved. The *bonum commune ecclesiae* is not theological but sociopolitical in origin.

The canonists of the School in Navarre have accepted the radical incapacity of the doctrine of "the juridical order" to resolve the basic theological problem of canon law. The first generation of them intended to pursue the technical and scientific work of their Italian teachers and colleagues by a further adaptation of the "general theory," especially in regard to constitutional law (*Lex fundamentalis*). Therefore, these canonists have felt the need to provide, in the postconciliar environment, a more solid theological infrastructure for canonical science. Not without a certain parallelism with modern Protestant doctrine, the canonists of Navarre have sought the *locus theologicus* in Christology and ecclesiology, taking as their central category that of "the people of God" (HERVADA and LOMBARDÍA), or that of the mystery of the Trinity (VILADRICH). The Italian positivist origin of the new attempt, nevertheless, has reemerged. The canonists of Navarre, using a monistic concept of law, have been forced to admit that, from the epistemological perspective, canon law is not a theological science, but a juridical one. The theological infrastructure, therefore, risks remaining a purely formal limit.

Canonistic doctrine would stay within this limit in order to avoid technical and juridical solutions irreconcilable with ecclesiology. The theological infrastructure does not affect the notion of canon law itself. Pedro Lombardia's dependence on secular juridical science explains how he can say that the central problem of the Church's constitution is that of defining the fundamental rights of Christians. This orientation of the School of Navarre seems not to be totally surpassed by its new generation of canonists.

Although some (Robleda, Bonnet) make strong arguments to the contrary, it does not seem that the extremely unitary system elaborated by Wilhelm Bertrams overcomes preceding methodological limitations, even though, as far as content is concerned, he abandons the well-trod paths of the *ius publicum ecclesiasticum* and of the Italian School in order to confront a clearly theological thematic. The fundamental theological assumption of his system emerges from a long Catholic tradition, namely, that which describes the Church as a human society elevated to the supernatural sphere (AYMANS). From the ontological and systematic point of view, the central point of the system consists of demonstrating that, in the Church as in any human society, the internal metaphysical structure cannot become actualized without the external sociojuridical structure, in the same way that the soul cannot become manifest in the person without the mediation of the body (GUND-LACH). The juridical dimension, therefore, comes from the external structure of the Church, and it is imposed by the fact that the internal structure of the human being tends to express itself in social forms — a concept universally acknowledged by philosophical anthropology. It follows that the unity between the internal and external metaphysical-sacramental elements of the Church is justified from a neo-Scholastic philosophical standpoint.

Thus, the natural law principle *"ubi societas ibi et ius"* reemerges under a different cloak. Indeed, the *external* structure not only poses the formal conditions for exercising law — already ontologically present in the *internal* structure of the economy of salvation and of the Church — but it creates that law, providing it with a real content. According to Bertrams, fundamental rights, rooted in baptism, are not only suspended in their exercise, but do not even exist when Christians place themselves outside the external juridical order established by the Church. Notwithstanding Bertrams' strong consciousness of canon law, the motivations he sets forth to establish a bond between Church and law remain on the level of philosophical methodology, not a theological one.

A theology of canon law that makes recourse to philosophy in order to provide the ultimate rational motivation for its existence is much weaker if metaphysical order is replaced by sociological order. While a methodological regression of this type is not possible within Protestant theology, it is taking place among Catholics, concurrently with the antijuridical positions of the postconciliar period, in the program of "de-theologization" and "de-juridicization" proposed by the journal *Concilium*. This program is founded on the principle of "the universality of the theological" and of "the relativity of the canonical" (ROUCO VARELA). According to Jimenez Urresti, it finds correspondence in formal logic because of the doctrinal character of theological language, which tends to offer definitions, and the pragmatic nature of juridical language, which tends to merely prescribe and provide practical judgments. This latter assumption is incorrect; it confuses juridical science, which certainly tends to provide definitions at the level of "general theory," with certain aspects of legislative technique.

This system, however, as it has recently been redefined by Peter Huizing, is founded on a doctrinal eclecticism that renders it incapable of providing a significant answer to the theological problematic posed by the ecclesial juridical phenomenon. According to Huizing, the function of canon law — defined by the category of "service" borrowed by Protestant theology (Calvin, Barth) — is to resolve the ever-emergent conflicts between the Church of love and the Church of law, between charism and institution.

Moreover, the capacity of canon law to *bind* Christians in conscience, without being able to *force* them — even through the institute of excommunication — is not motivated by a normativity intrinsic to theological reality, but by a neo-Kantian moralism that is unconnected with metaphysics.

Thus, the binding force of the canonical norm does not seem to be derived from the metaphysical and theological structure of the law itself because the ultimate normative source is not even constituted by the Church as institution, but by the Holy Spirit, to whom the fundamental function of the *discretio spirituum* is transcendentally attributed. Therefore, no juridical character is formally attributed to the notion of canon law, but merely that of being a function of order (*Kirchenordnung*). Its existence, moreover, is justified sociologically and on the basis of natural law, beginning with the consideration of its practical unavoidability because an ecclesial community that rejects "order" exposes itself to the risk of self-destruction.

The program of *Concilium*, without supporting itself by an explicit theory, tendentially reduces canon law to a purely extrinsic element. Canon law is postulated by the need for socioecclesial fellowship and held to be incapable of determining Christian existence intrinsically and structurally, except for the merely ethical plane. *Concilium* limits itself to pointing out, empirically, the dualism that exists between institution and charism, without attempting a response of its own, and entrusts the extrinsic task of resolving the ensuing conflict to ecclesial "order." Such an approach betrays too clearly a lack of logic in thought and method that does not enable this program to bear a theological analysis.

Contemporaneously with the attempts of Bertrams, of the School of Navarre, and of *Concilium,* some theologians and canonists have tried another methodological approach. They propose the mystery of the Incarnation as the theological *locus* from which to deduce an intrinsic relationship between the sociosacramental structure of the Church and canon law. As we have seen, the merit of identifying the insertion point of canon law in Christology belongs to Phillips and to his fascination with the new ecclesiology of the University of Tübingen. However, Phillips had seized only a partial aspect of this ecclesiology — namely that of the kingship of Christ — and had interpreted it within the parameters of secular public law. The Tübingen professors, on the other hand, tended to place the problem of the relationship of Christ, Church and society within the whole perspective of the mystery of Christ and of the Church. The mystery of the Church was considered to be the prolongation in history of the Incarnation of Christ.

The Tübingen insights were to remain unexploited for the better part of a century, until *Mystici corporis*, for several reasons. First, a historical and systematic preoccupation dominated the Pandectian study of canon law with Hinschius, Scherer and Wernz. Second, after the codification, an exegetical and manualistic pragmatism was prevalent within canonistic studies. The most important reason, however, was the modernist crisis, which contributed to keeping the academic prestige of the *ius publicum ecclesiasticum* intact until Vatican II.

Pre-Vatican II authors such as Salaverri, Stickler and Heimerl attempted to place the ultimate root of the social character of the Church within the mystery of the Incarnation of the Son of God. They affirm that Christ, by becoming incarnate, has taken on and involved himself with human nature in all its dimensions, including the sociocommunal one that is fulfilled within the Church (STICKLER). They also assert that such a root is suggested by the fact that the Church, as the historical moment of the working out of salvation, also continues to mediate Christ's intervention soteriologically, on the strength of the Church's normative imperativity (HEIMERL).

This methodological line, which attempts to overcome the extrinsic nature of alternative methodologies, has been approved by Vatican II, at least implicitly. In the constitution *Lumen gentium* (n. 8) and in the decree *Optatam totius* (n. 16), an indissoluble bond has been established between the

social and visible dimension of the Church as totality
of the mystery of the Incarnation and the existence
of the juridical dimension. Clearly, the doctrinal assumption of such a bond by the magisterium, even
if perfectly valid in content, has not been able to
render theoretically plausible the existence of law itself. First, the Council, not having redefined the
formal concept of canon law theologically, was forced
to borrow it implicitly from the social philosophy of
the Church. Second, if it is true that the mystery
of the Incarnation postulates the visibility of the
Church, then it is *not* true that such a visibility
necessarily postulates juridicity because, as Sohm has
held, such a visibility could also express itself through
a purely charismatic structure. It follows that juridical normativity is ultimately derived from the social
structure of human social life as it exists *before* its
assumption in the mystery of the Incarnation. The
imprint of natural law theory remains profoundly
present.

The terms of the problem do not change even if
the mystery of the Incarnation is substituted with
that of the presence of the Holy Spirit in the
Church, as was attempted by the magisterium itself.
(See the Address by Paul VI to the Second International Congress of Canon Law, 1973.) To resolve
this problem, it is not sufficient to affirm that "all
the juridical and institutional elements" — in the
same way, in any case, as the charismatic elements
— "are sacred because they are vivified by the Holy
Spirit," nor that "the Spirit and law, in their very
source, form a union," by which "the polarity between
the spiritual and supernatural character and the
juridical and institutional one of the Church, far from

becoming a source of tension, is always oriented toward the good of the Church, which is interiorly animated and exteriorly sealed by the Holy Spirit" (*L'Osservatore Romano* 1973, n. 213). This statement already *presupposes* the existence of ecclesial law. The juridical cannot be derived directly from the Holy Spirit without the institutional mediation of the Church.

It is impossible to avoid noting that these two methodological positions do not overcome either the theological dynamic — here reemerging between the lines — of the elevation of the Church as human society to the supernatural sphere, or the voluntaristic solution, according to which it is Christ and the Holy Spirit who directly will the juridicity of the Church. Nor would it be possible, clearly, to demonstrate that the juridical dimension of the Church is already present in the structural elements through which Christ and the Holy Spirit are present within, and give life to, the Church. As Christ and the Holy Spirit act in obedience to the specific modalities through which the Father has become manifest in history, we must ask why God has willed and chosen such modalities. Thus, the problem poses itself at an earlier stage and coincides with the ultimate question of every theological system, and the answer offered is always either realistic or voluntaristic. What must be avoided in specific cases is the acceptance for convenience's sake of a voluntarist solution that defines the existence of law in the Church, insofar as this is a particular problem, as dependent on the will of Christ, because it is impossible to offer another organic response internal to a fundamental theological option.

Avoiding both the natural law and voluntarist solutions inherent in the christological positions proposed by modern Catholic theology, Klaus Mörsdorf has sought the theological point of insertion of ecclesial law within the very elements that constitute the Church — that is, in word and sacrament. Word and symbolic sign, as primordial and structurally reciprocal elements of human communication, have always been used by world culture as fit instruments for the expression of juridical content. Christ, by placing himself within the dynamic of the history of salvation — in which God has already manifested himself through word and symbolic acts — has rendered explicit their whole binding force. And, by virtue of the Incarnation itself, Christ has impressed an ultimate value on word and sign — that is, a *sacramental* value in the fundamental sense of the expression. The word becomes kerygma and the symbol a sacramental sign of the presence of God. Word and sacrament address the most intimate part of the human person and require a response; by becoming incarnate, Christ has given the word and sacrament a definitive value for human existence.

In Mörsdorf's position, the key element of all Catholic fundamental theology emerges — that of the *locutio Dei attestans*. Against Sohm's Protestant doctrine, Mörsdorf enters into a direct polemic, reaffirming the thesis that word and sacrament do not bind humans to give their adhesion because of a subjectively perceived intrinsic truth, but because of the very fact that God has spoken and manifested himself. Word and sacrament, which therefore have a formal binding force, generate from their intrinsic structure a new form of social aggregation, destined to be the sign of God's presence in the world. Thus, the Church is a kerygmatic and sacramental community that has the same binding value globally as the word and sacrament from which it is genetically constituted. The incarnational principle finds its realization in the Church, even if it is not completely identified with Christ's Incarnation, through the mediation of word and sacrament, thus giving a primordial sacramental value to the whole ecclesial reality. The incarnational principle guarantees, therefore, the necessary relationship that exists between the Church and canon law.

Importantly, Mörsdorf identified a secure *locus theologicus*, even if not an exclusive one. More importantly, however, he applied a rigorously theological method, without making concessions to philosophical postulates. On the other hand, he leaves the problem of the formal theological meaning of the notion of law unresolved. That Mörsdorf has not resolved the problem satisfactorily emerges from the frequently cited definition of canon law he provides: *"eine theologische Disziplin mit iuristicher Methode."* If it is true that, in order to avoid the positivistic option, the method must be defined on the basis of the nature of the object and not vice versa, in what sense is it possible to apply the juridical method to a theological reality?

The Ontological and Epistemological Statute

The most lucid attempt to overcome this antinomy has been undertaken recently by Antonio Rouco Varela, one of the pioneers of the theology of canon law. Without pretending to provide a truly formal theological definition of canon law, the Salamanca canonist proposes a list of elements for the elaboration of the "ontological and epistemological" statute of ecclesial law and, therefore, also of the methodological one. The fundamental premise for isolating the ontological element from the theological perspective is that the problem should not be approached through the application of a philosophical preconception of the formal notion of law. Canon law, unlike secular law, is not generated by "a dynamism spontaneous ('biological') to human social life," but by the specific one inherent in the nature of the Church, whose social nature is genetically produced by grace and is knowable only through faith.

The second assumption at work here is that the problem of the juridical ecclesial phenomenon is not to be faced by focusing merely on one particular aspect of the mystery of the Church, such as Christ's "act of foundation," the categories "people of God" and "mystical body," Word and Sacrament. According to Rouco Varela, it is necessary to proceed progressively, taking into account all the essential connections that constitute the mystery of the Church. The first key moment is the definition of the Church as "people of God." This theological category is not meant to offer once more the possibility of justifying the existence of Church law by recourse to the natural law principle, *"ubi societas ibi et ius."* The importance of this category resides, rather, in the fact that it compels us to provide an anthropological meaning for the notion of "law" and allows us to avoid an excessive spiritualization of the *ius divinum*. Excessive spiritualization has been a problem for Protestant theology, from Luther to those modern authors who have sought a direct theological connection in the transcendental categories of Christology and of the mystery of the Trinity. Moreover, the fact that the Church, besides being "people of God," is also the "mystical body of Christ" offers the Christological element necessary to qualify the social and visible nature of the Church not on the basis of secular parameters — as Bellarmine had done in comparing the visibility of the Church to that of the Republic of Venice — but on the basis of the structure of the sacrament. The visibility of the Church is sacramental in nature.

Third, it is necessary to take into account the fact that the Church is a community founded on Word and Sacrament, whose ultimate binding force is addressed not only to the *homo interior*, but to the whole anthropological reality, internal and external, of the human person. Lastly, Rouco Varela underlines the impossibility, in evaluating the juridicity of the Church, of overlooking the principle of apostolic succession as guarantee of the present authenticity of the canonical injunctions of the Church. It follows that the "ontological statute" of canon law must be determined by beginning with its function of "expressing as a consequence of the Incarnation" the dimension through which the Church, as "sacrament of salvation in Christ," involves itself in a binding social manner, or with its function as "the structural dimension implicit in ecclesial communion."

Rouco Varela borrows his central methodological approach from Mörsdorf's work; nevertheless, his system is superior to the latter in two ways. In the first place, it has rendered explicit with extreme stringency the *status quaestionis* to which the theology of canon law must today provide an answer. The question is no longer merely whether the Church "tolerates law as an element determinant in its life, or whether consent is to be extended to it for more or less contingent historical reasons," or whether the Church needs law "because of a proper internal necessity as a community which lives a human condition, or because of sin." The question for Rouco Varela is, rather, whether "the Church as such, beginning with that by which it is positively constituted, needs law for internal necessity, that is, in order to be itself as sacrament of Christian salvation which lives of the breath of the Holy Spirit in faith, hope and charity." In addition, Rouco Varela has attempted to enlarge the perspective of reflection on the entire mystery of salvation as it becomes concrete within the Church, which is its definitive modality.

Although Rouco Varela does propose to return to the topic in a more analytic manner, it seems opportune to stress even now that a list of the constitutive elements of the ontological statute of canon law (people of God, mystical body, etc.) requires a detailed evaluation of the "specific theological weight" of each such element in the process of establishing the formal binding force of the ecclesial juridical phenomenon. In particular, it seems that the formal principle of apostolic succession presupposes the existence of Word and Sacrament. The Church is not juridically binding by force of the apostolic succession — to which, by diverse criteria, Protestant churches and even certain charismatic ecclesial communities can establish a connection — except in the sense that apostolic succession guarantees the authenticity of the juridical injunction already ontologically rooted in the fundamentally sacramental structure of the Church.

One of the most paradoxical results of Vatican II, whose subtle antijuridical vein might have raised other expectations, has been that of provoking a rigorous renewal of canonical science — a renewal which, nevertheless, theological science has not yet noticed. Within this renewal — which moves along several lines and is, in many ways, independent of the work of preparing of the new codification, — the formation of a new science of canon law begins to appear. This could lead canonical science, after the classical medieval one and the post-Triedentine one of the *jus publicum ecclesiasticum*, into the third phase of its history.

The first phase, having begun with Gratian's methodological and systematic distinction of canon law from theology, issued in the acknowledgement of canon law as the general science of law within Christendom, where the law of the Decretals, together with the Roman one, enjoyed the authority of common law. The *jus publicum ecclesiasticum*, formed as a new science after the Reformation, contemporaneous with the birth of the modern absolutist state of natural law origin, has developed a confessional juridical system whose primary function has been to guarantee apologetically the right of citizenship of the Catholic Church within the secularized cultural environment of the modern age.

Aside from the diverse methodologies followed, the fundamental tendency of postconciliar canonical science is to again provide the science of canon law with a more precise theological identity, which must necessarily issue in the elaboration of a juridical system exclusively conceived as an ecclesial juridical order — that is, as a law internal to the Catholic Church.

Within this perspective, both the cultural function exercised directly by medieval canon law on the development of the philosophy and general theory of law, and the apologetic function formerly performed by the *jus publicum ecclesiasticum* are indirectly reclaimed by the prophetic force of the theological datum enunciated by ecclesial law itself.

The first preoccupation of this new canonical science orientation has been to provide a theological justification for the existence of canon law, with a view toward elaborating a proper theology of canon law that cannot fail to touch on the question of methodology. Our analysis of the methodological approaches of Catholic canon law, from the mid-seventeenth century until today, in establishing the doctrinal presuppositions necessary to found the existence of ecclesial law in theology, clearly demonstrates how every attempt has remained incomplete. None has been able to establish a precise "theological statute" of canon law. The magisterium itself has provided indications that the problem of the theological foundation of ecclesial law must be faced within a global framework, namely, that of a theology of canon law (CORECCO). Moreover, the lack of a theology of canon law that can precisely fix the ontological and epistemological statutes and, consequently, the methodology proper to canonical science, will unavoidably render the present reform of the *Code, a priori*, merely interlocutory.

In effect, the problem is one of overcoming the methodological preconception from which this medieval formula polemically issued: *"Legista sine canonibus parum, canonista sine legibus nihil valet"* [A legislator without laws has little value; a canonist without laws has no value]. This reflects the cultural background of a Christendom in which the function of canon law was not limited to the ecclesial sphere, but extended also to the secular one because it pretended to contain a universal normative worth.

The "theologization" and "sacramentalization" of canon law do not lead to its "de-juridization" because the normativity that issues from the Church — as is evident in the institute of excommunication — is an unambiguous index of juridical authenticity, that is, of the existence of an injunction that binds the intersubjective relations of Christians as they face ecclesial authority and each other. Indeed, there exists no more strongly binding and imperative reality than the fact that God makes himself manifest to human beings through the historical concreteness of the Church. To attribute a formal juridical force to the reality of the Church is not merely to attempt a human conceptual approximation, but to intensify and render absolute the normativity of ecclesial law, at least in its founding elements, with respect to that of the state. Canon law has a binding force much greater than that of secular law, as it is more profoundly rooted in the normativity of the *ius divinum*, which is not primarily natural, but positive — that is, of revelation. In fact, it is a law that, unlike the secular one, does not pretend to require obedience at a merely ethical level; canon law goes to the very level of the ultimate and supernatural destiny of human beings and their salvation. It is, therefore, different from secular law in the whole totality of its elements, not only as a theological reality, but also as a juridical one.

In the same way that the theological reality of

canon law is also juridical, so its juridical reality is also theological without any possibility of dichotomy. This means that the theological reality does not so much oppose itself to juridical reality as such, but to a juridical reality that would pretend to be purely anthropological and rational. This suggests the defect of method that besets canonical science, namely believing that, having demonstrated the existence of the theological statute of canon law, it is still possible to treat it, from the juridical perspective, as a worldly reality. Canonical science must rigorously apply the theological method, leaving to the juridical one the role of a purely auxiliary discipline, as has been asserted by modern juridical science. The connection between divine law and the canonical human law can be established only within the logic and methodology proper to faith.

Even if the conviction has been diversely manifested, canonical science has always been conscious that, with respect to secular law, that of the Church is a *sui generis* law. Modern literature, however, goes further and begins to more stringently express the impossibility of continuing to consider secular law as *analogatum princeps* of the ecclesial one. Moreover, the use of the analogy itself begins to be questioned. If it allows negatively for the grasping of the diversity between the two juridical orders, it is insufficient to define positively the specific nature of ecclesial law and is even less fit to explain a general theory of more than juridical character, as has been amply done.

Inevitably, the search for a new ontological and epistemological statute of canon law brings to the fore the perennially key problems of juridical science:

those of the formal definitions of the notions of *right* and of *law*. It is significant that St. Thomas did not analyze the problem of law with the typical approach of the jurist or the canonist, but with that of the philosopher-theologian. Although he confronted only some essential elements of the question, he nevertheless noted the fundamental ones of the definition of *law* (I–II, q. 90 ff.) and that of *right* (II–II, q. 57). In addition, given that canonical science no longer wishes to define itself as a juridical science and but as a theological one, it must face the problem of the formal definition of its own subject *quod* — that is, of its own notion of law. Medieval and modern canonical science have defined law by starting with the category of *iustum* and of the *obiectum virtutis iustitiae*, but it is clear that these, being of philosophical origin, are not able to adequately explain the juridical dimension specific to the Church.

Canonical science can no longer be satisfied with handing down, without renewed examination, the notion of law underlying the CIC, formulated by Suárez as a synthesis of the entire philosophical-juridical thought of Scholasticism. Thus, the fundamental presupposition for a theological understanding of the ontological stature of ecclesial law is that we must not rely on a philosophical preconception of the fundamental notion of law. However, the need to avoid such a philosophical preconception does not mean, as Coccopalmerio seems to argue, that it is possible to derive the notion of canon law from an exclusive examination of the social structure of the Church. Given that the essence of the Church is knowable only by faith, such a process risks the failure of the *analogia entis*, rendering any theology incapable of finding a connection with reality and with history.

A prephilosophical and pretheological notion of law, in use in all human culture, allows both philosophers and theologians to engage in a reciprocally intelligible discourse, even if they use different definitions of law. Canon law, unlike secular law, is not generated by "the (biological) spontaneous dynamism of human existence," but by the specific social dynamism inherent in the very nature of ecclesial communion, whose sociality is genetically produced not by human nature, but by grace. Grace, then, establishes other intersubjective and structural relationships that are appropriate to the constitution of the Church and are knowable only through faith.

The ultimate end of the canonical order is not simply that of guaranteeing the *bonum commune ecclesiae*, but of realizing *communio*. Indeed, canonical order is the specific modality by which intersubjective relations and those relations that exist on a more structural level between the particular churches and the universal one become binding. The reality of the *communio*, therefore, has a binding force within the ecclesial community that goes beyond the potentially purely mystical limits of Eastern *sobornost*. It follows that the principle of *communio* must be considered as the formal principle of canon law — that is, of the *nova lex evangelii*, the starting point for defining the juridical structure of canonical institutes at both the formal and material levels. The ultimate juridical certainty of the canonical order, indeed, is not guaranteed by the *littera legis itself* — as happens with the order of the state, in which juridical *epikeia* is not possible — but from the *communio* that informs it. Thus, within the canonical system, one can speak of juridical certainty only by analogy. Moreover, if the point of reference were the modern state order, it would have to be denied.

The radical diversity existing between the *bonum commune ecclesiae*, understood philosophically, and *communio*, a theological reality founded in revelation, is qualitative — as qualitative as the gap that exists in the analogy between the *lex Moysis* and the *nova lex evangelii*, or grace. This gap is created by the fact that grace, having become ontologically "incarnate" in the human person, inserts the person in a new relationship with God and with other people — that is, into the relationship of *communion*. Thus, grace is the new and specifically ecclesial modality of the existence of the *ius divinum*, the root of a visible sociality different from all forms of merely human sociality. Further, grace is all the more binding, not only at the ethical but also at the structural level, because it claims to mediate salvation, or God's justice, by incarnating it and working through the institution "Church."

The problem of the nature of canon law cannot be resolved without a new formal definition of the concept of canon law itself. The CIC of 1917 and 1983 did not provide a definition of canon law, but many authors use the classic one of St. Thomas, "*quaedam rationis ordinatio ad bonum commune, ab eo qui curam communitatis habet, promulgata*" [ordinance of reason for the common good, promulgated by the one who has charge of the community] (II–II, q. 9 a. 4 c.), as the core and substance of their own definitions. Against the background of such definitions, however, there emerges a theology of the so-called "elevation," in which the Church is considered as a human society raised to the supernatural order. It follows that the ultimate point of reference of these definitions, despite the inevitable reference to revelation, is provided by the philosophical preconceptions of Christian thought with regard to human sociality and law. Therefore, it is not surprising that the state of the question has remained substantially identical with that posited by Thomas in the treatise *De legibus* in the *Summa*. Although waverings have been caused by emphasizing the element of the *voluntas* (with respect to the Thomistic definition centered around the *ratio*), there has been a preoccupation with clarifying the ecclesial or technical perspective of canon law with respect to Thomas's general definition of law.

The Thomastic definition is composed of four elements: reason, legislator, common good and promulgation. This definition is undoubtedly provided by the element *ordinatio rationis*. What did Thomas mean by defining the law as *ordinatio rationis*? One of the most complete and precise attempts to isolate the global meaning, within Thomistic theology, of the treatise *De legibus* (composed by Thomas in the full maturity of his thought) is undoubtedly that of the Protestant Ulrich Kuhn. Kuhn adopts a dialectical position in relation to other attempts. He does not limit himself — beyond the fact that he is not always successful in differentiating theology from *theologia naturalis* — to isolating the philosophical dimension of the treatise on law, but points out its theological value. We have come to share the opinion of Kuhn who, in line with Dempf and Grabmann, holds that the treatise *De legibus* represents the key point of

139

the entire ethic to which, in consonance with his general conception of the relationship between nature and grace, Thomas provides a greater breadth than that found in merely natural ethics. This ethic leads humans constantly toward their supernatural final end, the *beatitudo aeterna*.

The theological breadth of the treatise *De legibus* is especially evidenced by two elements. There is first the fact that St. Thomas, although he defines the law as *ordinatio rationis*, considers such a definition valid not only for human and natural law, but also for the *lex aeterna* and for the *lex divina*. As we have seen, the *lex aeterna* is a concept borrowed from Cicero through Augustine, who had already transformed it theistically, thus allowing it to become the central idea around which all medieval ethical-juridical thought gravitated. And, at the level of ontological and historical reflection, all other forms of law flow toward the *lex divina*. Indeed, the *lex nova*, prepared by the *vetus*, is considered to be the definitive form of the *lex divina* as the supernatural order of the economy of salvation. The *lex nova* clearly comprehends, assumes and reclaims the *lex aeterna* and the naturalis. In the *lex nova*, Thomas resolves the apparent antinomy between law and grace. Nevertheless, the ethics of the *Summa*, because of a more mature Aristotelian inspiration, reveal not so much a heterotheonomic starting point as an anthropological one. This preserves a transcendental and eschatological perspective, but it finds its basic presupposition in the affirmation of the natural ethical capacity of the human person, and it finds expression in the doctrine of the virtues, particularly the cardinal ones filtered through Aristotle from Plato.

This strongly anthropocentric premise emerges also in the treatise on law — considered to be an instrument through which God aids humans externally (I–II, p. 90, prol.) — in which Thomas takes his definition of law not so much from the eternal or the divine law, but from the human one that could be borrowed from the political models of the Christian and Roman traditions. Defining the law as *ordinatio rationis*, Thomas distances himself from the sacral and voluntaristic Franciscan tradition of St. Bonaventure (eventually taken up by Scotus and Ockham) in order to make a clear choice in favor of the *ratio*, anthropocentrically considered as the supreme principle of human acts (I–II, q. 9 a. 1 c.). Law does not bind through the force of a commanding will, whether transcendent or human, that demands obedience; rather, it binds through the rigor of a syllogism of practical human reason.

Although there is no theology of canon law in the *Summa*, it cannot be doubted that Thomas would have analogically applied his general definition founded on the *ordinatio rationis* to such a theology. Leaving aside speculations as to how he would have applied his general theory of law to canon law, it is clear that the fundamental problem of developing a theology of canon law is that posed by the central element of the definition itself — that is, by the *ordinatio rationis*. In what sense is the *lex canonica* an *ordinatio rationis*? We must place this within the context of a Christian culture in which Thomas could place all prelates, whether *temporales* or *spiritualis*, on the same level without causing any ambiguities. Thomas considered that all Christendom was ultimately to be ruled and governed by the *lex aeterna*, and the *ratio humana* was held to be, in fact, already informed by faith. To speak of the *ordinatio rationis*, therefore, did not create any problems, despite the emphatically rationalistic content of Thomistic Scholasticism. The most burning problem was not that of the juxtaposition of *ratio* and *fides* — given that the subordination of *ratio* to *fides* was acknowledged, and philosophy was peacefully considered as *ancilla* to theology — but the juxtaposition of *ratio* and *voluntas* within the pendular tension between the intellectualist and voluntarist traditions of thought.

In a cultural environment like the modern one, on the other hand, faith — not only insofar as it surpasses the force of human rationality, but also insofar as it informs rationality in order to help it fulfill its original function — is no longer accepted as a point of reference of the *bonum commune*. Rather, *ratio*, freed from all structural connection with faith, has become the ultimate and unappealable criterion of all human action. In such an environment, canonical science can no longer continue to define the *lex canonica* as *ordinatio rationis* without creating a gross ambiguity concerning its own scientific identity. The fact that this definition has been transmitted by modern canonical science — without bothering to stress its radically analogical nature — may not be surprising. In fact, until very recently, science either has taken the methodological approach of the *jus publicum ecclesiasticum* (whose primary reference point has ultimately been natural law), or the approach of the "general theory" (borrowed from modern juridical science), or that of exegetical canon law, which was never meant to go to the root of the problem of the theological nature of ecclesial law.

A canonical science that is called to give account of its own scientific identity, clarifying the ontological and methodological statute of its own *obiectum quod*, must be able to render radically explicit the analogical meaning that the Thomistic definition of law has for its own concept of norm. If the concept of *ratio* changes in meaning when applied to God — both because it loses all discursive value and because it no longer even preserves univocally the meaning of *intellectus* as affirmed in human cognitive potency (because in God the *intellectus* is affirmed only to be formally distinguished from *voluntas*) — then it is clear also that the notion of *ratio*, when referred to the *lex canonica* as the necessary human derivation of the *lex divina*, cannot preserve the same meaning it has in relation to the *lex humana*.

As understood in its primarily philosophical value, the *lex aeterna* corresponds to human positive law as *ordinatio rationis*. Understood in its primarily theological value, however — that is, as *lex divina revelata*, which is no longer the projection of human rationality or intelligence in God, but merely the incommunicable nature of the *intelligere* proper to God — the *lex aeterna* can no longer correspond to the *ratio* as a human discursive or intellectual modality but must correspond to another cognitive modality. The *ratio divina* — which, as we have seen, means *motivation* or *cause* (*Wesensgrund* or *Sinnstruktur*) of all realities contained in God's salvific plan — finds its *analogatum minor* not in *ratio* but in faith. Indeed, faith does not *know* through a person's discursive modality, which is motivated by the intrinsic demonstrative force of *ratio*, whether practical or speculative. Rather, the knowledge achieved by faith comes through accepting the authority of the *locutio Dei attestans* or of *gratia*. In faith, knowledge is not brought about by human logic; rather, the *ratio divina* itself is the ultimate "reason" or "cause" of all things. The *ratio divina* expresses itself *ad extra* as *ordinatio* or as the authority of God. Human persons participate in the *ratio divina* through *gratia*, or the infused supernatural virtue of faith. This means that they know the *lex divina*, define it historically and incarnate it in time, not by the stringent logic of the syllogism formulated by their own *ratio*, but by force of divine motivation or of the formal authority of the Word of God. The impulse of *gratia* leads human persons to accept that Word in the act of faith.

If it is possible, in the philosophy of law, to work with a notion of law that is metaphysically conceived as *ordinatio rationis*, by applying the *analogia entis*, then the proper analogy in theology is that of faith. It follows, therefore, that a general theory of canon law cannot be developed on the basis of a metaphysical definition of law in which a philosophical preconception of law itself is necessarily present. It follows, further, that the ultimate criterion of knowledge of the nature of law itself cannot be the *ratio humana*, but only faith. Faith operates at the level of human cognitive faculty. The existence of the *analogia* between *ratio* and *fides* is justified by the fact that, in both cases, a cognitive process is involved. The nature of this cognitive process of the faith, however, is profoundly different from that of human reason, even in its motivation or cause.

The analogy between *lex divina* and *lex canonica*, then, works on various levels: from below, as from *ratio* to *fides*; or from above, from the *ordinatio fidei* to the o*rdinatio rationis*. In the latter case, however, it is clear that the determinant element in the analogy is not the philosophical one of being, but the theological one of faith. This does not mean that canonical science, as a theological discipline, may exist without any connection to philosophical and metaphysical perspectives, as some branches of modern Protestant theology of law seem to believe. Although the *analogia fidei* is the fundamental epistemological criterion, this does not mean that one can do without the *analogia entis* in theology. It is one thing to note that natural law has too often become dominant over divine law, as with the *jus publicum ecclesiasticum* school, and to propose that this be limited to an exclusively ecclesial conception. The elimination of the *analogia entis* from canonical science, however, would be something else entirely. To substitute *fides* for *ratio* in the definition of canon law does not imply the elimination of the *analogia entis* as an epistemological criterion, as faith cannot be rooted in historical reality without this. This substitution simply postulates the elimination of natural law (or, in any case, its relativization), as a typical product of human rationality that may or may not be informed by faith, as an obligatory step in the process that creates the positive canonical norm.

The unity between positive divine law and human canon law need not necessarily be established by the mediation of natural law. In theology, the question is not, as in philosophy, that of establishing the intrinsic interdependence of divine law, rationally knowable under the name of *lex aeterna*, and human law, through the mediation of the *lex naturalis*. Rather, the problem is that of establishing an intrinsic connection between the *ius divinum positivum*, as a transcendent and supernatural divine reality knowable only through faith, and human canon law. Given that canon law is produced by the Church, it participates in the nature of the Church. And, although incarnate and immanent in history, *ius divinum* remains a supernatural reality knowable in its essence only though faith.

In terms of methodology, this means that the juridical method, as an expression of human rationality, cannot be applied autonomously to canon law, but only subordinately. However, this is also true for all the methodologies of the other human sciences, such as philosophy, natural ethics, exegesis, history or sociology, when they are treated as auxiliary sciences of theology. We must observe that this is not merely an extrinsic, but an intrinsic subordination of these disciplines to faith. Faith cannot be considered as a purely external boundary within which juridical science can move autonomously, as long as it does not trespass beyond the limits of theology. Such a methodology would allow canon law to be treated as a secular reality.

For canon law to remain an authentically ecclesial reality without secular compromises, faith must be the ultimate principle that intrinsically informs its method. Philosophy's function is to elaborate the *preambula fidei*, seeking to understand and intelligibly develop the rational noncontradictory nature of revealed truth. Likewise, juridical science's function is to elaborate positive canonical norms that

allow us to understand the rational noncontradictory nature — that is, the rationally binding value
— of the *ius divinum*, knowable only through faith.

Canon law must be defined as *ordinatio fidei* because it is not produced by any one human legislator but by the Church, whose decisive epistemological criterion is faith and not reason. Further, as
a human and historical knowing subject, the Church
is endowed with human rationality, socialized not
according to human criteria but according to the
modality of the *communio ecclesiae et ecclesiarum*.
It follows that the Church's human rationality remains intrinsically informed by faith, because the
Church's function is not merely to produce a juridical order that is compatible with the philosophical
concept of justice, but to produce an order derived
from the theological notion of *communio*. In this
order, the dynamics of the institutionalization of
intersubjective relationships is radically different
from that of any merely human social reality.

The priority of faith over reason is not realized
only when the Church discovers or acknowledges
the supreme principles of the *ius divinum*, on the
strength of its charism. The priority is also realized
when the Church applies itself to the "incarnation"
of these principles in the particular historical, social
and cultural situation in which it lives, by means
of positive juridical norms and by making use of the
lumen rationis — that is, or the juridical method.
Indeed, there can be no dichotomy between the
epistemological level of the supreme principles and
the operative level where concrete juridical norms
are produced, because there is no dichotomy between

the spiritual and the sociological Church. The unity of epistemology and praxis around the principle of faith distinguishes the Church from all other knowing subjects and distinguishes the canonical method from all other human juridical methodologies.

Bibliography

Afanassieff, N. (1960). "L'Eglise qui préside dans l'Amour," in *La Primauté de Pierre dans l'Eglise Orthodoxe,* Paris-Neuchâtel.

Aymans, W. (1966). "Papst und Bischofskollegium als Träger der kirchlichen Hirtengewalt. Gedanken zu einer Schrift gleichen Titels von W. Bertrams," in *Archiv für katholisches Kirchenrecht.*

Aymans, W. and Mörsdorf, K. (1991). *Kanonisches Recht, Lehrbuch aufgrund des Codex Iuris Canonici,* Band I, Paderborn-München-Wien-Zürich.

Alivisatos, H. S. (1932). "Das kanonische Recht in der orthodoxen Kirche," in *Ekklesia X. Die orthodoxe Kirche auf dem Balkan und in Vorderasien,* Gotha.

Althaus, P. (1956). "Die beiden Regimente bei Luther. Bemerkungen zu Johannes Heckels Lex Charitatis," in *Theologische Literaturzeitung.*

Barth, K. (1955). *Die Ordnung der Gemeinde. Zur dogmatischen Grundlegung des Kirchenrechts,* München.

Bertrams, W. (1969). *Quaestiones fundamentales iuris canonici,* Roma.

Beth, K. (1902). *Die orientalische Christenheit der Mittelmeerländer,* Berlin.

Bidagor, R. (1947). "El espiritu del derecho canónico," in *Revista Española de Derecho Canónico.*

Bulgakov, S. (1959). *L'Orthodoxie,* Paris.

Clément, O. (1965). *L'Eglise orthodoxe,* Paris.

Coccopalmerio, F. (1977). "De conceptu et natura iuris Ecclesiae. Animadversiones quaedam," in *Periodica de Re Morali Canonica Liturgica.*

Congar, Y. (1972). "Propos en vue d'une théologie de l'"Economie" dans la tradition latine," in *Irénikon.*

Corecco, E. (1987). "Paul VI et le statut du droit canonique," in *Paul VI et les réformes institutionelles dans l'Eglise*, Brescia.

Daniélou, J. (1944). *Platonisme et théologie mystique*, Paris.

D'Avack, P. (1956). *Corso di diritto canonico*, Milano.

De La Hera, A. (1967). *Introducción a la ciencia del derecho canónico*, Madrid.

De La Hera, A., and Munier, C. (1964). "Le droi publique ecclésiastique à travers ses définitions," in *Revue de Droit Canonique.*

Dombois, H. *Das Recht der Gnade. Oekumenisches Kirchenrecht I*, Witten, 1961; *II*, Bielefeld, 1974.

Dumont, P. (1937). "Economie ecclésiastique et réitération des sacrements," in *Irénikon.*

Ellul, J. (1948). *Die theologische Begründung des Rechts*, München.

Evdokimov, P. (1965). *L'ortodossia*, Bologna.

Fassò, G. (1970). *Storia della filosofia del diritto*, Bologna.

Fedele, P. (1962). *Lo spirito del diritto canonico*, ebd.

Flückiger, F. (1954). *Geschichte des Naturrechts; Bd. 1, Altertum und Frühmittelalter*, Zollikon-Zürich.

Fuchs, J. (1955). *Lex naturae*, Roma.

Ghirlanda, G. (1975). "Il diritto civile "analogatum princeps" del diritto canonico?" in *Rassegna di Teologia.*

Gundlach, G. (1943). "Annotationes in Nuntium Radiophonicum Pii XII, 24.12.1942," in *PRMCL.*

Hamel, E. (1987). "Epicheia," in *Dizionario Enciclopedico di Teologia Morale*, Milano.

Haring, J. (1899). "Die Lehre von der Epikie," in *Teologischpraktische Quartalschrift.*

Heckel, J. (1953). *Lex Charitatis*, München.

Heiler, F. (1937). *Urkirche und Ostkirche*, München.

Heimerl, H. (1966). "Aspetto cristológico del Derecho canónico," in *Ius Canonicum.*

Hervada, J., and Lombardia, P. (1970). *El Derecho del Pueblo de Dios, I*, Pamplona.

Holstein, G. (1928). *Die Grundlangen des Evangelischen Kirchenrechts*, Tübingen.

Huizing, P. (1967–68). "Delitto e pena nella Chiesa," in *Concilium*.

Iwand, H. J. (1962). "Protestantismus," in *Evangelisches Kirchenlexikon III*, Güttingen.

Joest, W. (1961). "Gesetz und Evangelium," in *Evangelisches Kirchenlexikon I*, Göttingen.

Karmiris, J. M. (1972). "Abriss der dogmatischen Lehre der orthodoxen katholischen Kirche," in *Die Orthodoxe Kirche in griechischer Sicht, I–II*, Stuttgart.

Kölmel, W. (1953). "Das Naturrecht bei W. Ockham," in *Franziskansiche Studien*.

Kotsonis, H. (1972). "Die griechische Theologie," in *Die Orthodoxe Kirche in griechischer Sicht, I–II*, Stuttgart.

Kühn, U. (1965). *Via Caritatis. Theologie des Gesetzes bei Thomas von Aquin*, Göttingen.

Lanne, D. E. (1962). "Le mystère de l'Eglise dans la perspective de la théologie orthodoxe," in *Irénikon*.

Lau, F. (1962). "Zwei-Reiche-Lehre," in *Die Lehre Luthers*, Tübingen.

L'Huillier, P. (1969). "Le divorce selon la théologie de l'Exarchat du Patriarche Russe en Europe," in *Le Message de l'Exarchat du Patriarche Russe en Europe Occidentale*.

Liermann, H. (1933). *Deutsches evangelisches Kirchenrecht*, Stuttgart.

Lombardia, P. (1973). *Escritos de Derecho Canónico, I–III*, Pamplona.

Louvaris, N. (1972). "Kirche und Welt," in *Die orthodoxe Kirche in griechischer Sicht, I–II*, Stuttgart.

Manser, G. M. (1944). *Das Naturrecht in thomisticher Beleuchtung*, Freiburg i. Ue.

Martini, L., and Ippoliti, A. (1971). "Sondaggi a proposito dell'attuale dibattito sui fondamenti teologici del diritto canonico con particolare riferimento al progetto di lex ecclesiae fundamentalis," in *Testimonianze*.

Meilia, E. (1970). "Le lien matrimonial à la lumière de la

151

théologie sacramentaire et de la théologie morale de l'Eglise orthodoxe," in *Le lien matrimonial,* Strasbourg.

Mörsdorf, K. (1989). *Schriften zum Kanonischen Recht,* Paderborn-München-Wien-Zürich.

Ott, G. (1952). "Recht und Gesetz bei Gabriel Biel," in *Zeitschrift der Savigny-Stiftung für Rechtsgeschichte,* Kanonistiche Abteilung.

Pannenberg, W. (1961). "Gnade," in *Evangelisches Kirchenlexicon I,* Göttingen.

Phillips, G., *Kirchenrecht I–VII,* Regensburg, 1955; Graz, 1959.

Prenter, R. (1961). "Eschatologie," in *Evangelisches Kirchenlexikon I,* Göttingen.

Rapaport, M. W. (1913). *Das religiöse Recht und dessen Charakterisierung als Rechtstheologie,* Berlin-Leipzig.

Robleda, O. (1947). "Fin del derecho en la Iglesia," in *Revista Española de Derecho Canónico.*

Rommen, H. (1947). *Die ewige Wiederkehr des Naturrechts,* München.

Rouco Varela, A. (1973). "Le statut ontologique et epistémologique du droit canonique. Notes pour une théologie du droit canonique," in *Revue des Sciences Philosophiques et Théologique.*

Rouco Varela, A., and Corecco, E. (1971). "Sacramento e diritto: antinomia nella Chiesa?" in *Riflessioni per una teologia del diritto canonico,* Milano.

Sauter, J. (1932). *Die philosophischen Grundlagen des Naturrechts,* Wien.

Schilling, O. (1914). *Naturrecht und staat nach der Lehre der altern Kirche,* Paderborn.

Schönfeld, W. (1943). *Die Geschichte der Rechtswissenschaft im Spiegel der Metaphysik,* Stuttgart.

Schüller, B. (1963). *Die Herrschaft Christi und das weltliche Recht. Die christologische Rechtsbegründung in der neueren protestantischen Theologie,* Roma.

Seeberg, E. (1949). "Das Christentum," in *Religion der Erde,* München.

Sohm, R. (1892). *Kirchenrecht I,* München-Leipzig. (Berlin, 1970).

Söhngen, G. (1947). *Gesetz und Evangelium*, Freiburg-München.

Steffes, J. P. (1932). *Das Naturrecht in metaphysicher und religiöser Weltsicht*, Augsburg.

Steinmüller, W. (1968). *Evangelische Rechtstheologie. Zweireichelehre-Christokratie-Gnadenrecht, I–II.* Köln-Graz.

Stickler, A. M. (1962). "Das Mysterium der Kirche im Kirchenrecht," in *Das Mysterium der Kirche II*, Salzburg.

Stiegler, A. (1958). *Der kirchliche Rechtsbegriff*, München.

Thomson, F. J. (1965). "Economy," in *Journal of Theological Studies*.

Verdross, A. (1963). *Abendländische Rechtsphilosophie, I–II*, Wien.

Viladrich, P. J. (1969). *Teoría de los derechos fundamentales del fiel*, Pamplona.

von Balthasar, H. U. (1972). "Le tre forme della speranza oggi," in *Communio*.

von Campenhausen, H. (1965). *Die Begründung Kirchlicher Entscheidungen beim Apostel Paul*, Heidelberg.

Wehrhan, H. (1951). "Die Grundlagen problematik des deutschen evangelischen Kirchenrechts 1933–45," in *Theologische Rundschau*.

Wenzel, H. (1951). *Naturrecht und materielle Gerechtigkeit*, Göttingen.

Wittmann, M. (1920). *Die Etik des Aristoteles*, Regensgurg.

Wolf, Erik. (1961). *Ordnung der Kirche. Lehr — und Handbuch des Kirchenrechts auf ökumenischer Basis*, Frankfurt.

Zankow, S. (1946). *Die orthodoxe Kirche des Ostens in ökumenischer Sicht*, Zürich.

Index

Abelard, 33, 40
Afanassieff, N., 63, 65
Albert the Great, Saint, 34
Alexander of Hales, 32
Alivastos, H.S., 71
Althaus, P., 87
Ambrose, Saint, 25, 26, 34
Anselm, Saint, 32
Antigone, 6
Aristotle, 10, 18–21, 28, 93, 140
   metaphysical foundations of
   law and, 15–20
Augustine, Saint, 29, 30, 50, 51
   102, 108–09
   unity of law and, 26–28
Aymans, W., 120

Barth, K., 97–102, 103, 104,
   106, 107, 108, 122
Beatitudes, 88
Bellarmine, 130
Bertrams, W., 119, 120–21, 123
Beth, K., 61
Bidagor, R., 119
Biel, Gabriel, 43, 47, 85, 93
Bloch, E., 56
Bonaventure, Saint, 33, 40, 141
Bonn Constitution, 96
Bulgakov, S., 65

Calvin, John, 81, 91, 98–99,
   106, 122
Canon law, 21–30, 57–58,

108–48, 121, 122
Catholic theology and, 111–19;
De Legibus and, 135–47; divine
will and, 39–42; dogma in,
70–77; grace and law, 108–12;
methodological developments,
112–28; ontological statute,
128–48; and ontological/
epistemological statute, 128–48;
philosophical implications,
120–28; and Protestant
theology, 101–09; Protestant
versus Catholic views, 110–13;
Thomistic analyses, 35–39,
135–48; trinitarianism and,
103–05, see also Law
Castro, 52
Catholic theology, 5–15, 57–58,
108–48 and Canon law,
111–19; divine will and, 39–42;
dogma in, 70–77;
epistemological issues, 128–48;
faith and knowledge, 135–37;
grace and law, 108–12; "Loci
theologici" of Canon Law,
103–05; methodological
developments, 112–28; natural
law and, 25–26; ontological
statute, 128–48; rationality as
source of, 43–48; salvation and,
112–13, see also Canon Law;
Divine law; Law; Orthodox
theology

155

157

About the Author

Eugenio Corecco is Bishop of Lugano, Switzerland, and has been adviser of the Papal Council for the interpretation of the legislative texts since 1984. He has also served as chair of the *Consociatio Internationalis Studio Juris Canonici Promovendo* since 1987. Formerly, he was professor of canon law at the University of Fribourg in Switzerland.